WOMEN OF GRACE

by Jennifer Mathewson Speer

OUTCOME
PUBLISHING

Women of Grace

Published by Outcome Publishing
8007 18th Avenue West
Bradenton, Florida 34209
www.outcomepublishing.com

Unless otherwise indicated, Bible quotations are taken from The Holy Bible, New American Standard Version. Copyright © 1960, 1962, 1963, 1968, 1971, 1972, 1973, 1975 by The Lockman Foundation.

First Edition

Printed in the United States of America

1. Religion: Spiritual General
2. Self-Help: Spiritual
3. Religion: Christian Life – Personal Growth

In loving memory of
Dr. Dana Patrick Mathewson
Our loss. Heaven's gain. Grace through it all.

This book is dedicated to my mother
June Mattheiss Cosby
The ultimate example of grace in trials

CONTENTS

Forward

Esther Burroughs

"Its hard to be a woman in another woman's shadow. It is quite another thing to be a woman in the shadow of the Almighty."

Jennifer's book, *Women of Grace, Broken Lives that Lead to Hope*, is a study of eight women in the lineage of Christ who are, by grace, in the shadow of the Almighty. Just the title of this book will draw you close enough to discover it is written for women like you and me. As you read this book, like me, you may be weeping over Tamar's story of grace or laughing with Sarah over the angel's announcement or seeing new insight into Mary's story. Regardless of the chapter, I promise you will find yourself standing beside these women as you see God's touch of grace in their lives. You will see yourself as well as truth covers your heart and soul, knowing we too are part of God's story. Jennifer says, "Every woman has a broken place in her life which God can cover with His grace, using it to lead others to hope."

It has certainly been a delight knowing Jennifer since she was a college student. She is a beautiful, radiant woman, full of His presence. She writes from a deep well of joy and pain, sharing with the reader how God sustains.

WOMEN OF GRACE
Introduction

I love to read. But rarely do I spend much time on the preface, table of contents, or introduction of a newly selected book. Instead I usually skip it all and get right to the good part.

I tend to approach Scripture the same way, gravitating to the familiar passages, the comforting verses and the chapters I understand. I skip long lists of hard to pronounce names, numbers in armies, sundry laws and generally anything that would challenge my five minute attention span. Until one day I was asked to bring a Christmas message for a women's event.

No problem, right? But this particular church had already heard all of my Christmas messages. In fact, I had been there a dozen times and they had heard everything I had ever studied, written or thought. I needed something fresh and new. I needed to hear from the Lord. It wasn't going to be easy, since as a widow, I had just remarried a widower with three children and relocated my two children from Tennessee to Illinois. We were in the process of trying to get these two grieving families merged into one and now, in the midst of it all, I had to figure out what to say at a women's Christmas event.

I decided to read every passage of Scripture that had anything to do with the birth of Christ. The familiar ones came first—Luke, Isaiah, Micah, Matthew......Matthew. Hmmmm—starting with verse 18 of the first chapter things look familiar. But back up just a bit and it is one of those tedious lists of names. A genealogy. I had never tackled a genealogy before but this one caught my eye and my heart. God's Spirit said slow down and soak it in.

Forty-six names, forty-two generations, two thousand years of history and the unusual addition of women. Matthew is Jewish, writing to Jews, clearly establishing that Jesus is the anticipated Jewish Messiah. But women? Why include women? They were not normally included in Jewish genealogies and yet there they are—five of them. Three others, Sarah, Rebekah, and Leah, are silently present by the inclusion of their husbands. Eight women—three of the eight are not even Israelites.

As I examine the list more carefully, I begin to recall the stories behind the names. Not one is pristine. It seems that every name in the list except for Christ himself, struggled with something. In fact, this genealogy is a broken road of tangled and sinful people that apart from grace would lead nowhere. Instead, it somehow leads to Jesus. Of the 46 souls, those eight women grab at my heart. Their inclusion broadcasts the fact that Jesus is the Savior for all, and God's grace is sufficient for everyone, even women—even women like me.

Those thoughts lead me to further explore the lives of these women and the truth God has for us today. November of 2006, a Christmas message emerged entitled *There's Always Hope*. A single message led to an expanded study, *Women of Grace*. It has become one of my favorite studies in these years following my late husband's tragic death and more recently, my cancer diagnosis. Through deep brokenness, I have more intimately experienced the grace of God though Christ. I love this study and these women because I am one of them. A woman deeply marred by sin, often crippled by circumstances but oh so covered in the precious grace of the Lord.

It is my prayer that this study will encourage you to see yourself, no matter what your background or baggage, as a woman of grace—a grace that will lead you to hope in Christ.

1

SARAH
Laying Down Your Burdens

Have you ever felt like God was not coming through for you? Have you prayed and grown weary of waiting for someone or something to change? Have you lost hope and perhaps taken matters into your own hands? Has it affected your relationship with God? And with others?

Sarah is a woman who loses sight of hope. She tries to manage a situation that is not hers to manage. She carries a burden no one laid on her rather she took it upon herself. She frets, stews, calculates and ends up creating one of the biggest messes in history, the consequences of which we still reap today.

Grace intervenes.

I never expected to be a widow at 45. I never thought my perfect life as a pastor's wife and mother of two sons would crash in around me. I didn't know I could be so broken. After all, I had been a minister's wife for 20 years; I was a seminary graduate, a Bible teacher, a conference speaker. I knew all the right answers and most assuredly, I knew the Lord. Yet in the months and years that followed our tragedy, I made some of the worst decisions of my life. Some decisions were made in grief and loss. Some were made in sin and anger. Many of my choices have had a profound effect on my boys, my own life and even the man who would become my husband. For several years I struggled under the weight of some of my choices, the guilt and fear debilitating.

Grace intervenes.

The resounding message of hope Scripture gives for me and for every other woman who has tried to manage her own life and made a mess is that *God's grace is bigger than our choices.*

Listen carefully. God's grace is given to us at great cost, made available to you and me through the death and resurrection of Christ. God's grace is not permission to live any way we choose or make any flippant decision that crosses our mind and then ask God to fix the consequences. We cannot be reckless with our lives and then slap Romans 8:28 over it like a huge spiritual Band-Aid and say, "Ok God, fix it. Make it work out for good."

The Apostle Paul makes it very clear that we come into a personal relationship with God by grace through faith in Jesus Christ. *"For by grace you have been saved through faith: and that not of yourselves, it is a gift of God; not as a result of*

14

works, that no one should boast" (Ephesians 2:8-9). We do not deserve this relationship. We did not do anything to earn it. We can't even muster up enough faith to receive it on our own. Scripture says we were dead in our trespasses and sin (Ephesians 2:1). Dead things can't respond unless the Spirit of God quickens us to respond. Therefore each and every aspect of our salvation is based on God's grace. God draws us to Himself—by grace. God quickens us to be able to respond—by grace. God offers us a relationship with Him—by grace. This relentless grace is made available *to us* because of what Christ has done *for us*.

Grace is God's favor toward us, a favor we cannot earn and we do not deserve. Most of us understand our salvation is by grace but we do not recognize every day of the Christian life is sustained by grace. We are dependent on it for everything! Most of us don't like being dependent. We want to add something of our own making to grace. And we are not the first. The church in Galatia was trying to add to grace. Yes, they were saved by grace, but someone persuaded them they also must obey a bunch of rules and laws. Paul writes them a letter to correct this thinking. Doctrinally, it reiterates the book of Romans, but Paul is hot under the collar when he writes Galatians. *"You foolish Galatians, who has bewitched you....having begun by the Spirit, are you now being perfected (matured) by the flesh?"* (Galatians 3:1a & 3). Crazy. Impossible. Following rules, coming up with laws, living apart from grace and somehow thinking this is the Christian life. It is treacherous and defeating, but we do it too! We do it every time we try to take control of our own lives.

Living apart from grace has two extremes. The first extreme is legalism. If I follow all the rules, then I am in good standing with God. If I go to church, give money, eat right, live clean, look the part, then certainly I am living the Christian life in excellence. This kind of living is exhausting. No amount of discipline can make me holy. Legalism is also problematic because other people become my measuring stick. I gauge my goodness by others' goodness or lack of goodness. Either pride or insecurity will be the governing force of my life if I am living by rules. It will drive me to performance based Christianity—proud of myself when I succeed, self-loathing when I fail and in the end, angry with myself and everyone else. I have never met a Christ-like legalist.

The other extreme is license and it is just as dangerous. It is living with complete disregard for God's holiness, doing whatever feels right at the time, and then somehow expecting God to fix it all when it comes crashing in. It is saying, "God is so good and so gracious and so loving that He will forgive me and make it all right." Paul addresses this line of thinking in Romans 5 and 6, *"...but where sin increased, grace abounded all the more....What shall we say then? Are we to continue in sin that grace might increase? May it never be! How shall we who died to sin still live in it?"* License is what some theologians refer to as cheap grace—a grace we take lightly and flippantly, disregarding the great cost to God.

Truthfully, most Christians live somewhere between these two extremes. We want to do what is right, but we sin. We want to live victoriously, but we make foolish choices. We want to move forward, but we stumble. We want to trust God, but we take charge of our own lives.

Knowing we are weak and sinful and yes, even hopeless, how do we become women of grace? How can you and I rest in God's wonderful grace? The answer can be summed up in one word. Surrender. Paul teaches us the essence of surrender when he refers to himself as a *doulas* or bond-servant of Christ. A bondservant is defined as one who is in a permanent relationship of servitude, his will abandoned to the will of the master. Sarah would eventually learn the lessons of grace and surrender but only after watching her efforts to control everything around her crumble.

Scripture Introduces Sarai

What do we know from Scripture about Sarah? When she is introduced to us, her name is Sarai which means "my princess." She is the wife of Abram and she is also his half-sister. She and Abram have the same father, Terah, but different mothers. (Before we recoil at that thought, we must remember the history of mankind is young, the gene pool is not exceedingly polluted and the marriage laws of God are not yet written in stone.)

Sarai is a city girl growing up in Ur, one of the most advanced civilizations in the ancient world. She is 65 years old when she first appears on the pages of the Bible and no matter what her age, she is always described as extremely beautiful. Her beauty would be both a blessing and a curse and probably because of it, she has been a little pampered. At times she is manipulative. She has a temper and she can even be vengeful.

Her beauty however, cannot compensate for the fact that she is barren. To her, this condition is the most painful and even shameful aspect of her life. It produces more insecurity than any amount of beauty can offset and it certainly navigates almost every event of her life.

But more than any fault we might find in Sarah, two overwhelmingly wonderful characteristics stand out. First, is her complete devotion to her husband Abraham, and second, is her tried and found true faith in God.

Sarah's Devotion to Abraham

From the very beginning of the narrative, Sarai is faced with circumstances that would unsettle most women. God tells Abram to leave his home, take his family and go to the land that God would show him. Not a lot of specifics. God gives no information about how they would live, where they would live, or if they would ever return to friends and family in Ur. Abram obeys and Sarai does not argue when they pack their bags to depart.

For me this is huge. Every time my husband has even considered a move, I dig in and become unmovable. I hate change. I like my house, my nest, my friends, my church. I want all the answers before the For Sale sign ever touches the front yard. But not one word of resistance is recorded from Sarai. This is even more remarkable when we realize that Sarai never again had a permanent home. She was a nomad, living in a tent until the day she died. And she never complained. Why? Because she is completely devoted to her husband Abram. She will go where God sends him and she will do whatever it takes to remain faithful and loyal to him. In fact, in all likelihood, it is this unflinching loyalty to Abram that is at the root of her great compromise in Genesis 16. She wants what God has promised for Abram's sake.

While Sarai is undyingly devoted to Abram, Abram is less than careful with her loyalty. No sooner than their feet leave Ur and enter Egypt, Abram, the man of faith, waffles. His concern is Sarai's beauty. Poor guy—what a burden! He is afraid his own life will be jeopardized because the Egyptians will kill him in order to have her.

So godly Abram devises a plan to save his own neck while compromising his devoted wife. He tells Sarai to say she is his sister. After all, it is partly true. They had the same father so technically she is his half-sister. In doing this however, he abdicates his role as her husband and her protector. He obviously fails to depend on God in the whole episode.

More amazing than Abram's neglect, is Sarai's willingness to honor Abram's request. Sometimes the Bible is devoid of emotional details. I would like to have heard Sarai's first response to that idea of passing her off as his sister. "Are you out of your ever lovin' mind?" would top my imaginative list of responses. Instead of arguing, she walks into Egypt pretending to be only Abram's sister.

True to Abram's fears, the Egyptians notice the beauty of Sarai and take her to Pharaoh's house. Evidently, the ruler had intentions of making her his wife or at least his possession. Abram on the other hand prospered in the whole web of deceit, gaining livestock and servants in this supposed exchange. I always wonder what Abram was thinking at this point. "How am I going to get out of this charade alive? If Pharaoh does not kill me, Sarai will!"

God intervenes.

The Lord's mercy and grace rescue Sarai, but her rescue is framed in judgment against Pharaoh. Plagues befall his household. The ruse is discovered and Abram and his wife are escorted out of town taking with them everything Pharaoh had given them. It is a demonstration that the ruler wanted to be rid of them and he did not want any other consequences of their deception to affect him. Good riddance.

I have to stop at this point and ask the Lord what we are to learn from this debacle. Did Sarai trust her husband's judgment so much that she blindly obeyed him? Was she naïve? Did she know that God had her back no matter what her husband did? I don't know. I just know God's grace and God's mercy stepped in at the right time.

You will read a dozen times in this book, "God's grace is bigger than our choices." We make choices every day. Some are made in sin. Some are made in innocence and naïveté. Some are made with the best intentions but have the worst outcomes. Some are made with limited knowledge of consequences and outcomes. But no matter the motivation behind our decisions, when we lay them at the feet of Jesus, confessing our limitations, and taking our hands off-—God's grace is more than adequate to cover our choices. His grace covers even the consequences of our choices and brings glory to God while also working together for our good. As a matter of fact, God's grace can work in our lives even before we get to the point of surrender, before we realize we have blown it and made a foolish choice. His grace is always at work in our lives.

His grace, His mercy and His sovereignty also work together for us when someone else's choices are affecting us adversely. Abram's choice to lie had adverse consequences for Sarai. But God never dropped his watchful eye over Sarai. Sometimes we cannot escape the choices of others. Our husband, our employers, our government will be wrong sometimes. Our lives are often caught in the crosshairs of someone else's decisions. God's grace is not a place to become passive and accept everything that comes down the pike but it is a place to rest when we are at the mercy of something beyond ourselves. God is caring for us and working on our behalf even if others are not. His grace, mercy and sovereignty are never an excuse to live sloppy, disobedient lives. Rather they are compelling realities that constrain us to live in surrender to Him.

Whether Sarai is blindly obedient and naïve or whether she trusts God with her husband's shortcomings, we will never know. But the fact remains, God stepped in on her behalf regardless of Abram's choices. That's grace at work. It is at work in your life too. It is cause to stop and be thankful for the loving grace of the Father made available to us through a relationship with Christ. As if salvation were not enough, His ever working grace is reason for us to bow daily in surrender to Christ.

Sarah's Faith

The most troublesome aspect of Sarai's life is childlessness. The problem is complicated by the fact that God has promised to make Abram the father of a great nation through his biological descendants (Genesis 12:7 & 15:4). What is she to do? She is barren. There is no hope of God blessing Abram through her. And so Sarai picks up a burden that is not hers to carry. She begins to feel responsible for making God's promise come true. Somehow she believes sovereign Almighty God needs her help to accomplish His purpose.

Before we are too hard on Sarai, let me remind you we do it all the time. As women, we carry burdens that are not ours to carry. We feel responsible for raising perfect children, reforming our husbands, meeting everyone's expectations, always being the peacemaker, never disappointing anyone. We know God's ideal but we somehow think our striving, our worrying and our working will accomplish it in our own lives and in the lives of those we love. Oddly enough, much of our striving is rooted in love and good intentions but leads to heartache. Any time we lay our hands on what only God can accomplish, disaster is sure to ensue.

I cannot begin to tell you all the plans I have concocted in an effort to accomplish something I was sure was God honoring. I am guilty of manipulating circumstances and pretending it is God at work. The result is always a lack of peace and shortsighted results with no eternal fruit.

Dear one, there are things only God can do in our husbands and our children. There are relationships only the Lord can soothe and mend. There are people who can be molded and changed only by the supernatural work of the Holy Spirit. There are events which cannot be undone by our striving. There are homes that can only be healed with His balm. There are hearts whose only cleansing can come from Christ's forgiveness. Lay down your burden of fixing it all. Get out of the way and let God go to work.

A Costly Failure

Sarai made a grave mistake when she stepped into the role of God. Her sin cost her dearly and set into motion consequences that rock our world even today. In an effort to see God's promise for her husband come to fruition, Sarai brings another woman into the picture. How crazy is that? (We do crazy things when we usurp God's place.)

Hagar is an Egyptian slave, probably acquired when Sarai and Abram made their first trek through Egypt. She may be one of the spoils Abram received when pawning his wife off as his sister. Regardless, Hagar belongs to Sarai and Sarai chooses to give her to Abram as a slave wife. It was a common practice in ancient times. The offspring of the slave was considered a child of the owner of the slave. Sarai owns Hagar so Hagar's child will really be Sarai's child. See how nice and neatly that works out? A simple, unemotional, no strings attached answer to the dilemma of childlessness. I hope you hear the sarcasm.

It was not God's intent. It was not God's plan. It was a human attempt to carry out God's divine purpose. So when Hagar becomes pregnant with Abram's child and then ridicules her barren mistress, Sarai throws a jealous fit. Her harsh treatment of Hagar sends that pregnant vamp packing, across the blazing desert and home to Egypt. Indignant, Sarai fully expects Hagar to die in the wilderness, getting rid of a prideful slave and the disaster she carries in her womb, getting rid of the consequences of Sarai's own solution to God's promise. What a mess! What a miserable unintended outcome to well laid plans and good intentions. Yet God's grace prevails.

I am so thankful God does not walk away from me when I have made a mess of things. I am so thankful He can use even the consequences of my sin to bring glory to Himself. His grace is bigger than my choices and I am amazed. There is no circumstance beyond the reach of God's grace. There is nothing too difficult for His intervention no matter how royally I have messed it up. His grace, however, is not an excuse to continue in the mess. Neither is it a dismissal of consequences. Grace is an opportunity to bow in humble submission and surrender to the Almighty and His plans. It is a chance to finally and forever realize that God's plans cannot be thwarted, nor can they be accomplished in our own strength.

My husband of twenty-one years, Dana Mathewson, died as a result of a car accident in 2005. The blink of an eye trauma changed life forever. At the time, our boys were ten and fifteen. While I had always considered myself a stable person, strong in my faith and dedicated to my family, the two years following Dana's death proved to be anything but stable. I made some decisions that had a profound effect on my sons—especially the oldest. These choices were not made with any malice or rebellion in my heart and I did not foresee the consequences those decisions would yield. But in making them I watched my oldest son suffer.

There is no guilt like that of a loving mother who has wounded her child. The grief of losing my husband coupled with the guilt of wounding my son was inconsolable. I wept before the Lord day after day, month after month, year after year. I tried to undo the damage I had done, only to cause more damage. Despair set in.

This is why I love Sarah so much. I see myself in her story. I see decisions made in good faith that yield disaster and the despair that quickly follows. I know, first hand, the mess can fester even more when human hands try to undo and accomplish what only God can orchestrate. And I, like Sarah, watch in amazement as

Grace intervenes.

As the crisis in my heart and the crisis in my oldest son's life reached a crescendo, the Lord clearly said to me through the Spirit and the Word, *"My grace is bigger than your choices."* He began to clear out the fog and show me anew the depths of His grace. My pit and my son's pit were so very deep but His grace proved even deeper. The Lord assured me of His great love for my son. Through Scripture, He reminded me His plans for my son could not be thwarted by my choices. His sovereignty trumps my limited scope every time—even in the lives of my children. I did not have to be a perfect mother, making perfect decisions in order for the Lord to mold my son into a Godly man. He also reminded me that my worth as His child was not diminished by this difficult season of life. He assured me of His redemption of all I had chosen in ignorance and His forgiveness for all I chosen in sin. The guilt lifted.

Every decision we make, good or bad, produces an effect or a consequence. So while the truth set me free from guilt, the consequences and effects of my actions remained. Certainly the Lord can make it all work together for good but the process is not always instantaneous. For me and for Sarai there would be a season of waiting.

A Season of Waiting

Thirteen years pass between Genesis 16 and Genesis 17. Sarai must wait and watch. Because God spared Hagar in the wilderness and sent her back to Sarai, Sarai must watch another woman's son grow up in her household. She watches him take his first steps and say his first words and she sees her husband Abram thrill at each passing accomplishment. She witnesses her husband's heart being gladdened by the very presence of this young life and she knows the attachment of father to son has nothing to do with her or her body or her ability to bring life into the world. The weight of barrenness has not lifted but the lesson of meddling in God's place has been learned.

And Sarai waits. She waits for God to fulfill His promise in God's way and in God's time. She waits for God to redeem the consequences of her hasty actions.

Not many of us enjoy waiting. We like instant answers and quick resolutions. Waiting seems so passive and we like action. But is waiting really passive? Is it a season of sitting on our hands and doing nothing? Psalm 37:3-4 gives us direction while we are in a season of waiting.

*"Trust in the Lord and **do** good; **dwell** in the land and cultivate faithfulness. **Delight** yourself in the Lord; and He will give you the desires of your heart."*

Three phrases all beginning with the letter "d" will help us turn a season of waiting into a season of actively obeying and looking for God to work.

Do good

The psalmist says we are to trust in the Lord. Trust is visible. It is not simply mental assent to truth rather it is living in that truth. If we trust the Lord, if we are confident that He is all that He says He is, there will be proof of that trust in our everyday lives. The first measurable proof of trust is "doing good". This is not good works. To "do good" means to be obedient. Soon after Dana died, a friend who I greatly respect said, " Jennifer, do what you have always done." She meant, keep walking with God. Keep praying. Keep reading your Bible. Keep fellowshipping with believers. Keep serving. Keep living an obedient life. Bad or unusual circumstances do not change the basics of our relationship with God through Christ. Circumstances do not negate the everyday routine of the Christian life.

Seasons of waiting for the Lord do not give us permission to lie down and do nothing. We are not allowed a pity party while we sit on our hands and wait for God to change everything. Get up, girl, and by the power of the Holy Spirit within you keep walking, keep being obedient, keep doing good! It demonstrates you are trusting.

Dwell in the land

Dwelling in the land also proves you are trusting. *To dwell* means to settle down and live there. The writer of Psalm 37 is encouraging the people of Israel to remain in the land God has given them. Even in the lean years, even in the turbulent years, even in the uncertain years, they are to stay put! Huh? Is Scripture saying God wants us to settle down and stay in a bad place? If God is not changing the circumstances in our lives, then His intention is to change us in the midst of our circumstances. James 1:2-4 states that difficult circumstances produce in us endurance, the ability to remain under the circumstance while God works out His plan in and through us. Psalm 37 tells us that remaining in the land—whatever the land is and however we got there—cultivates faithfulness in us.

"Cultivate" is an agricultural word. Farmers and gardeners cultivate. My sister cultivates. She can grow anything. Karen can take a dead looking plant and nurture it back to lushness. Her back porch is evidence of her green thumb. I, on the other hand, can't grow anything but weeds. My houseplants almost reach out and grab me begging for a drink of water. I easily forget about them. But not so for my sister. She fertilizes and prunes. She places the plant in just the right spot for sun or shade. She knows how to keep the birds or the squirrels from ruining it. She digs in the dirt and replenishes the soil as needed. She cultivates and cultivating takes time. The result, however, is a strong, beautiful, healthy plant that gives pleasure to everyone who sees it.

If God is requiring you dwell in the land of your present circumstances then you can be assured He is cultivating you. He may prune and cut back. He may dig in the dirt or place you in the hot sun. He may do things that seem unpleasant in your life. But ultimately He is doing a good work in you. He is making your roots go deeper and your leaves flourish. He is making you into a strong, healthy follower of Christ who gives off the fragrant aroma of Jesus to everyone around her. Let God do this in you while you wait, while you trust, while you dwell in the land.

Delight in the Lord

Thirdly, while we are waiting and trusting, as evidenced by doing good and dwelling in the land, we are also to delight in the Lord. Quickly reading Psalm 37:4 we are usually drawn to the second phrase, *"...and He will give you the desires of your heart."* Amen! That's what I've been waiting for—for God to give me what my little heart wants. Right? Hardly.

We cannot disconnect the two phrases of verse four. To delight ourselves in the Lord literally means to become pliable in His hands. It means we let God mold us and change us through whatever means He chooses. As He molds us into Christlikeness, the desires of our hearts will change as well. Our desires will line up with His desires. God is free to give us the desires of our heart because our desires now reflect the things He wants. Our desires match His desires because we are delighted in the Lord, pliable in His hands.

Sarai had to wait thirteen years to see God's promise come to fruition. But while she waited, God did the same work in her that He wants to do in you and me. He deepened and cultivated her faith. He assured her of His great faithfulness and ability to keep His promises. He used the uncomfortable circumstances of her life to mold her into a woman who would be the mother of the child of promise.

Dear woman, have you put your own hand to circumstances or the lives of people you love and in doing so, made a mess? Have you been assured that God's grace is indeed bigger than your choices but now you must wait while He redeems it all? Lay it all at His feet. Confess your shortcomings and His sufficiency. Give up control. Trust Him and do good. Dwell in the circumstances He has allowed and through it all, let Him deepen your faith and make you into the woman He desires you to be.

Waiting is not passive. It actively trusts God, who has promised to never leave us or forsake us. For me, the wait was six years. I prayed with the broken heart of a mother waiting for her prodigal to come home. Never once did the Lord abandon me. Never once did He leave my son. I could not heal the wounds in my child but the Lord could.

Grace would intervene.

A Promise Fulfilled

Sarai is the only woman in Scripture whose age is revealed (Genesis 17:16). Presumably, her age is given so that we know without a doubt, childbearing is physically impossible. It does not matter that people lived longer in those days; her old age still presents an impossibility to reproduce. Her physical limitation is exactly what God is waiting for. For Abram and Sarai having a child is impossible, but with God nothing is impossible.

Abram is ninety-nine years old when the Lord speaks to him again. This time God introduces Himself as El Shaddai, God Almighty. The name means all sufficient, or complete and perfect. This elderly couple could not produce a child. In fact, Paul says in Romans 4:19 that Abram *"contemplated his own body which was as good as dead and the deadness of Sarai's womb."* The circumstances are humanly impossible, yet El Shaddai is enough. He is sufficient and He is perfect and complete to meet the need. The impossible melts into hope.

For the first time, God attaches Sarai's name to the promise. This time, there will be no doubt that hers is the womb the Almighty will use to raise up a nation. She will be the mother of the promised son and in that confirmation God changes her name from Sarai, *my princess*, to Sarah, *princess*. No longer did she just belong to Abram but she was now the princess of God. Abram's name is changed as well. He is called Abraham from this point on in all of Scripture. The changes in their names identify them with Yahweh, the promise keeping God.

We are changed when we encounter El Shaddai. Certainly our lives changed when we met Christ and we were saved by grace. But as believers, when we walk through the difficulties of life and experience the hand of El Shaddai at work, we are marked by His presence. Others may look at us and see suffering, or trials and burdens, but each crisis is an opportunity for God Almighty to display His sufficiency. God is actively working in and through the impossible situations of our lives. Through them, He is maturing and completing us, marking us with Christlikeness and identifying us with the promise keeping God.

Finally, Sarah hears for herself the promise of a son with her name attached to the promise! The angel of the Lord visits Abraham at the door of his tent. They share a meal and partake of ancient customs. All the while Sarah is inside the tent, listening. This is not the manipulating woman of previous chapters. This is an old woman about to explode with excitement. God is at work. She can sense it. She hears the visiting messenger say *"Sarah, your wife, will have a son"* (Genesis 18:10). She knows it is impossible. She knows she is old. She knows Abraham is old. Maybe she remembers the last time they tried to get cozy and it was a disaster. She chuckles to herself at the remembrance.

I used to read this passage with a somber tone. The Bible lets us do that you know—imagine the tone of a situation or the emotions of the people. I call it using my sanctified imagination. They are, after all, real people with real feelings and Scripture rarely tells us what they are feeling. So I imagine. I used to think the angel was stone faced and stern, warning Sarah not to be so happy. After all this is a holy announcement.

But in recent years, I view Sarah's inner laugh as joy that cannot be contained. I no longer think the messenger poked a long a boney finger at Sarah and said, "Straighten up woman, this is no laughing matter." And I do not believe Sarah was scoffing at God or mocking her husband and the messenger. It seems she was truly overflowing with excitement and she was smiling on the inside as she pondered the impossibility of it all. The angel calls her on it to prove he is divine and he can actually read her thoughts. He uses the moment to reiterate nothing is impossible with God. Mull over the messenger's question. *"Is anything too difficult for the Lord"* (Genesis 18:14)? Hundreds of years later, another angel would use almost those exact words to tell another woman she will have a baby under impossible circumstances. (See Luke 1:37) Nothing is impossible with God.

What circumstances can you lay that phrase over like a blanket of hope? Dear one, God is not giving us permission to claim any outcome we choose. We do however have a blessed hope and assurance that whatever God promises, He will do. Sarah is through coming up with her own plans. She has waited thirteen years, learning to trust. She is now brimming with gladness and anticipation because she finally hears her name attached to the promise. There is great hope because there is great grace being demonstrated toward her.

For the first time in the narrative of Abraham and Sarah, God reveals a timetable for the events that will unfold. The angel says, *"At the appointed time"* and then clarifies by saying, *"this time next year Sarah will have a son"* (Genesis 18:14). The writer of Genesis uses the same phrase in Genesis 21:2, *"at the appointed time."* It simply means at the right time, at God's designated time.

The Lord does not work on our timetable. He has His own sovereign plan and His own timing for everything. I cannot manipulate, beg or cajole the Lord's timing. My pastor often says, "God is never late and rarely early." God is on time. His time. His way. His plan. My wise dad and I were discussing the perfect timing of God one morning at breakfast. I was waxing eloquent and he was listening. Then true to his style, my dad summed up the whole issue of God's sovereign timing with a few words. "Yes, but sometimes He will scare you to death." And the Lord does scare us to death sometimes. I am not always patiently and faithfully waiting for the Lord to work. Many times I am wringing my hands and begging Him to hurry. But God will not be rushed.

In Abraham and Sarah's case, The Lord God, El Shaddai, would magnify the weight of His words, *"Is anything too difficult for the Lord?"* by waiting until indeed everything was impossible with man. He waited until Abraham and Sarah were physically incapable of producing and conceiving a child. He waited until the ancient couple had relinquished their own plans and surrendered to His. He waited until no one but God Almighty would get the glory. God even protected the wait through Abraham's treacherous second indiscretion of Genesis 20. Nothing would alter the hand of the Lord in fulfilling His promise of a child and ultimately making a great nation of Abraham and Sarah.

By the time that blessed baby Isaac arrives, all of Sarah's worries have melted. All of her waiting has come to fruition. All of her insecurities have been crushed. All of her hopes are fulfilled, not because Sarah is a perfect woman of faith but because God is a great God of grace and she the recipient of His grace. Oh the joy and humble thankfulness that follows the realization of God's grace at work. Even the name Isaac, which means "laughter," beams with joy and gladness at this occasion of grace.

Certainly we are saved by grace, but precious believer, we also live by grace. Every blessing bestowed, every answer to prayer, every promise fulfilled, and every treasure that is ours in Christ is because of God's grace towards us. We do not have the outpouring of God's grace because we are perfect examples of Christians. We have grace because of His faithfulness to us even in our imperfections.

The response to such great grace is humble surrender. It is the declaration of total dependence on Christ. Not our way, not our plan, not our timing but His. Not our sufficiency, but His. Not our lives but His. It is a daily surrender and a daily acknowledgment of our need for His grace. Our response is a daily, sometimes hourly, abandonment of our will for His.

I have often heard people misquote Scripture and say God will never give us more than we can handle. Of course He does! If we could handle it, why would we need Him? Our Lord will not step in as long as we think we have the strength, resources and ability to handle the circumstances of our lives. But when we finally come to the end of ourselves and become dependent on Him, El Shaddai, God Almighty, goes to work. He cares deeply about every need in our lives, but He will not share His glory with us. When all else is impossible, He alone receives the honor and glory.

Sarah is Remembered

Sarah's joy in bearing Isaac quickly turns into her need to protect Isaac. Sarah makes a final demand of Abraham. She demands that her husband drive out Hagar and her son Ishmael. Ishmael, a young teenager, jealously mocks Isaac. Sarah will have none of it. Cast out that woman and her son!

It seems harsh to us. It seems harsh to Abraham. He has grown to love his firstborn son, Ishmael. But God, in grace, promises to spare the boy's life and to make him a great nation; even though Ishmael is not the child of promise, he is indeed the son of Abraham. On a personal level, God so loved the world… and Hagar and Ishmael are part of the world. They would be recipients of God's care. On an allegorical level, Hagar and Ishmael represent the law and man's inability to save himself.

Paul uses the analogy of Sarah and Hagar in Galatians 4:21-31 to point the church toward grace. Our relationship with God through Christ cannot come by our own good works. Sarah gave Hagar to Abraham, trying to work out the plan of God in their lives. The child produced was a result of human works, not divine intervention. Ishmael had to be cast out along with Hagar because they would always represent man trying to work out God's plan without God. On the other hand, Sarah, in her old age, hopelessly barren, becomes pregnant by her hopelessly impotent husband Abraham. The child produced is miraculous. God's grace at work in their lives is the only explanation. Isaac is a picture of our salvation –God at work, providing through grace our salvation in Christ.

Dear one, perhaps you are a good person by most people's standards. You have tried to live a good life. You are honest and loyal. You attend church. You are generous with money. But without Christ, without God's grace, all these wonderful actions are like Sarah trying to achieve God's promise on her own. It can't be done.

We are all sinners. None of us can meet the standard of salvation on our own. We all deserve to be cast out like Hagar and Ismael. Romans 5:8 says *"But God...."* (I love it when Scripture says, "but God." It tells us grace is about to step into a hopeless situation.) *"But God demonstrated His own love toward us, in that while we were still sinners, Christ died for us."* God does not wait until we are good. He sent Christ while we were sinners, hopelessly barren and impotent, incapable of saving ourselves.

The Old Testament always points us toward the New Testament. Sarah points us toward grace. Her final years are a beautiful picture of God at work, fulfilling His promise by grace. She is remembered by New Testament writers as a devoted wife, loyal to Abraham. She is also listed in Hebrews 11 as a woman of faith. God revealed His plan, and Sarah believed God. This is faith. This is Sarah.

In closing this first chapter, let me ask a few questions. Is there anything in your life you are trying, by your own power, to fix? Are you trying to manipulate circumstances to get the outcome you desire? Are you stepping into a role only God can occupy? Do you trust the Lord with your imperfect husband? Your wayward children? Your difficult circumstances? Your broken relationships? Are you weary of waiting for things to change? Are you anxious about the future?

Be encouraged. God is still El Shaddai. He is still God Almighty. Nothing is too difficult for Him. Take your hands off. Relieve yourself of the responsibility to fix everything and everybody. Rest in the grace offered by Almighty God. Do good, dwell in the land, delight in the Lord, while He works on your behalf simply by grace.

I am not free to tell my oldest son's story. It is his to tell someday. But I can tell mine. I am a woman who has experienced great grace. Grace for salvation, yes, but also grace that covers the things I tried to fix and manipulate and would finally have to surrender to the Lord.

The night of Dana's death, God tenderly directed me to Matthew 7:25. *"And the rain descended, and the floods came and the wind blew and burst against the house; and yet it did not fall, for it had been founded upon the rock."* Our home had been dedicated to Christ from the beginning. Dana and I had made a conscious effort to build it upon Christ the Rock. On this night, however, the storms had burst against our blessed home. Yet even in the howling winds of death and grief, God promised that the house founded on Him would not fall. Ten years later, by grace, the house still stands.

Two years ago, I sang *Amazing Grace* at the wedding of my oldest son and his beautiful bride. It was the most appropriate song ever. *"Through many dangers, toils and snares, they have already come. Tis grace that brought them safe thus far and grace will lead them home."* [1] At the wedding, I sat by Allen, my husband of seven years, while the minister read words written by my late husband, Dana. I marveled at the goodness of God. The tears flowed.

Grace prevails.

Oh precious woman, as you trust Him with the difficulties of your life: as you look to God as the one who meets your needs: as you rest in the promises He makes available to us in Christ, you like Sarah, will see yourself as God sees you. A woman of grace.

For Group Discussion

1. The recurring theme of this book is, "God's grace is bigger than our choices." Yet often, Christians try to live apart from God's grace. The result is usually one of two extremes, legalism or license.

What is "performance-based" Christianity or "legalism" and why is it a dangerous way of living?

Ignoring God's holiness and living however we choose is "license". Why is this way of living equally as dangerous for Christians?

2. In Genesis 16, Sarai picks up a burden that is not hers to carry. Why is she wrong in her choice to help Abram become "Father of nations" as God promised? What are the consequences of her choice?

How can we avoid this sort of mistake?

3. Sarai waits thirteen years before she sees God's promise fulfilled. Have you ever experienced a "season of waiting"? Why might this season be important in our own lives?

Read Psalm 37:3-4. How did "doing good," "dwelling in the land," and "delighting in the Lord," mold Sarai? What might these truths mean for our lives today?

4. Read Genesis 17:1 and 18:14. Ponder these three truths.
a. God is Almighty, El Shaddai.
b. Nothing is too difficult for the Lord.
c. "At the appointed time" is God's perfect timing.

In light of these three truths, why is the advanced age of Sarah and Abraham of special significance?

What is the lesson for us as we apply these truths to our own circumstances?

5. Read Genesis 17:18-21 and Genesis 21:9-21. On a personal level, how does God demonstrate His care for Hagar and Ishmael?

Read Galatians 4:22-23 and 28. On an allegorical level, how can we apply the story of Ishmael and Isaac to our own salvation?

Read, ponder and memorize Ephesians 2:8-9. Why is being a religious person not enough to achieve salvation?

2

REBEKAH
Finishing Strong

Finish Strong. My friend has these words tattooed on her wrist in her late husband's handwriting. It was his mantra, his life message which he lived victoriously even as cancer ravaged his body. My friend has it tattooed on her wrist as a visual reminder, even in her husband's absence, to finish life strong. Unfortunately, not every believer in Christ will finish strong. There are bumps along the way from which some never recover. Grace, however, is still present and grace is still at work.

Rebekah is the second woman in our study. She is one of the unnamed yet silently present women in the Matthew 1 lineage of Jesus. She is the wife of Isaac, daughter-in-law of Abraham and the eventual mother of twins. Her home and her family are the centerpieces of her life. She begins well and there is much to learn from her and admire about her.

Sadly, Rebekah does not finish strong. Her failures emanate from the very thing most important to her—her home. Yet she can still be considered a woman of grace. She is still part of that broken road of names in Matthew that leads us to Christ who is our hope. Even though Rebekah has failures, God does not have failures. His grace remains, in spite of her shortcomings and ours. His plan and His promises, then and now, will be fulfilled, not because we are perfect but because He is faithful. There is as much to learn from Rebekah's failures as there is to learn from her successes. Rebekah is a recipient of grace because God's promise of creating a nation for Himself would be fulfilled through her son, even though by her own doing, she would never have the joy of seeing it.

Qualities to Admire

The story of Rebekah begins in Genesis 24. Abraham is an old man and his son Isaac is not yet married. No parent wants to depart this earth without first making sure their children are cared for. Abraham is no different. He sends his most faithful servant to find a wife for Isaac. The servant must first promise to never let Isaac take a pagan wife but instead to find a woman among Abraham's relatives who knows the God of Abraham. The servant agrees and sets out.

The faithful servant does three important things. First, he prays, asking God to bless the endeavor of finding a wife for Isaac. At the same time, he takes a hefty dowry with him. Third, he has a plan to make his camels kneel beside a well in the evening when the women would come to draw water. There the servant waits and watches for God to work.

We can like this guy. We would be wise to follow his pattern. Sometimes we think we are supposed to pray and then sit on our hands waiting for the miraculous. Perhaps the Lord works that way at times, but not often. The servant moved forward with a plan, trusting God to direct him and prepared with a dowry for God's answer. Rebekah is the answer God gives the servant.

Rebekah is young, beautiful and unmarried. So far so good. But there is more. Rebecca is kind and industrious. There is a sense of hospitality about her. She draws water for Abraham's servant and for his camels too. She is not afraid to work. What admirable qualities in a young woman. The servant silently observes her, discerning if this is the woman for his master's son. The answer is sure when Rebekah identifies herself as the daughter of Bethual, a member of Abraham's extended family. In humble thanksgiving, the servant bows low and worships God. His praise to the Lord is voiced in Genesis 24:27.

Rebekah hurries home, bringing the servant with her, and tells her family about the events at the well. She is now part of a bigger story and greater plan. Oh the thrill of knowing she is part of God's design. Her brother Laban tries to delay her and milk the servant of more riches, but Rebecca will have none of it. She knows God is at work and she agrees to leave immediately with Abraham's servant.

Mark it down. Rebekah shows great faith. Faith is not a leap into the dark. It is a step into the light God has given. Rebekah believes the servant. She trusts God's plan. She leaves everything behind to go with the servant, sets out in faith and I think her heart was soaring. The anticipation of meeting a wealthy man's son, the nervous flutter of becoming a wife, the joy of knowing she is God's choice in it all makes the long journey seem effortless.

The meeting of Isaac and Rebekah is tender. It seems to be love at first sight. It certainly is a well suited marriage. The Bible says Isaac loved Rebekah and she in turn comforted him in the loss of his mother. In a culture that often included multiple wives and concubines, which were secondary wives, Isaac never took another wife or concubine as long as he lived. He loved Rebekah and Rebekah only.

Rebekah loves her husband as well and wants to bless his home with children but she, like Sarah, is barren. Her circumstances are different than Sarah's because Rebekah's barrenness seems to be short lived. Isaac wisely goes to the Lord in prayer. Genesis 25:21 is an understated verse but filled with truth. The loving couple has a problem and Isaac takes it to God. God hears and answers. Rebekah becomes pregnant.

So far, there is a pattern of prayer surrounding Rebekah's life. The servant prayed and she is the answer. Her husband prays and God allows her to conceive. So when there is a problem with the pregnancy, Rebekah follows the pattern and turns to the Lord in prayer. It is one of her most admirable qualities. As a matter of fact, everything in her life up to this point is admirable. She is a woman of beauty and faith, an industrious woman in a loving marriage, taking her burdens to the Lord. I wish we could just stop right here, make a Hallmark movie, get out our hankies and say they lived happily ever after. But we can't and they didn't.

Warnings to Heed

Children changed everything for Isaac and Rebekah. During her pregnancy, there was a struggle in her womb. When she asked the Lord why this was happening, His answer is prophetic. The turmoil inside of her is actually twins from which two nations will emerge. One nation will be stronger than the other and the older brother will serve the younger. No way! That can't be right. The first born is always the leader, the one who inherits, the one who carries on the family name even if this child is the first born by only a few minutes. The prophecy would haunt Rebekah.

Indeed twin boys are born. Esau is the first born and Jacob the second, though Jacob is born grabbing the heel of his older brother. The Bible describes them as very different in appearance and temperament. In fact, one is like Isaac and one is more like Rebekah. Each parent had a favorite. Isaac loves Esau who is robust and industrious—like Rebekah. Rebekah loves Jacob who is a peaceful indoors man like his father, Isaac. Curious isn't it, that mother and father are drawn to the child who is most like their spouse?

Favoritism disrupted the once peaceful home. Proverbs 11:29 says, *"He who troubles his own house will inherit the wind."* And oh how the winds of trouble blew. Each boy seems to be affected differently by his parent's favoritism. Jacob remains close to home, tied to his mother, increasingly deceitful. Esau resents his parents as well as his rights and responsibilities as the oldest. He sells his birthright for a bowl of stew, despising all it represents. He marries two pagan women and the Bible says in Genesis 26:35 these women brought much grief to Rebekah and Isaac. The fabric of home is torn.

Rebekah began as a woman of great faith, but as Genesis 27 unfolds the tide has turned. Her sons are grown, Isaac is old and it is time to pass the torch to Esau, the oldest. The words that Isaac will speak over Esau are binding. They are the last will and testament of the father to the son. There is no changing destiny after Isaac speaks his blessing.

In her mind, the prophecy of years earlier weighs heavy as does her heart, pulled in favoritism toward Jacob. Rebekah does not pray. She does not seek God's answer to the seeming dilemma of the prophecy. She acts, and like Sarah, she takes it upon herself to help God out. She will force the words of the Lord to come about by her own devices. Jacob will be the heir. He will be the stronger. God said so. Rebekah stops trusting God. The results are similar to Sarah's. Disaster.

With secrecy, deceit and manipulation, Rebekah puts the final nail into the casket of a dead marriage and a dysfunctional home. She concocts a plan to trick Isaac into blessing Jacob instead of Esau. Her lies are parallel to unfaithfulness. Her indulgence of Jacob creates further division, alienation and strife between brothers. The grief of it all never wanes.

Esau bears a murderous grudge against his brother. In hate and anger he runs to the person who can cause the greatest heartache and destruction to his father. He runs to Ishmael, the son of Hagar, the outcast child of his grandfather Abraham. The Bible says that when Esau understood the Canaanite women in Ishmael's territory displeased his father Isaac, he married two more of them. "In your face, dad!" He hates his father. He hates his brother and mother. Esau is just biding his time, waiting for Isaac to die so he can murder Jacob.

Rebekah never repents of her deceitful actions. Instead she tries to soothe the consequences by sending her precious Jacob away to her brother Laban's house. Rebekah dies never seeing her beloved son again. She never sees the promise fulfilled in his life. She never sees the blessing of Isaac bear fruit in Jacob. She dies a joyless woman, tired of living, vaguely a shadow of her admirable beginnings.

Lessons to Learn

I feel like I have just written the Cliff notes to some tragic, depressing novel. But it's Scripture. The Bible never whitewashes the lives of people it presents, which give us the opportunity to learn from their missteps as well as their victories. There is much to glean from Rebekah's life.

We would be wise to learn that no matter what season of life we are in, our walk with the Lord matters. Whether you are a mom of preschoolers or a grandmother; an aunt, sister or daughter; widowed, single or married, your relationship with Christ is the most important aspect of your life. It affects everything you do and every relationship you have—especially in your home.

Rebekah started so well. She had faith, she trusted God, she sought the Lord in prayer and she followed Him without question. But she failed in mid-life. This is an important observation. It was not the sins of youth that tripped her up. She had walked with God a long time. She knew better than to engage in behavior that would rip her home apart. So why did she?

Interestingly, most of the great sins in Scripture happen in midlife. Moses was not a young man when he disobeyed God and struck the rock. His sister Miriam was not youthful when she sinned and spoke against her brother and God disciplined her with leprosy. Aaron was not a teenager when he fashioned a golden calf and caused the people to stray. David was not a youngster when he sinned with Bathsheba and murdered her husband to cover it up. Solomon was not a new king when he took foreign wives and built altars to their foreign gods. All of these people had walked with God for many years. They had experienced a relationship with the Almighty in wonderful and exciting ways, and then they sinned greatly in midlife.

While we were in seminary, my late husband Dana had a part-time job with a construction crew. Construction really was not his strong suit, but it paid the bills and gave him a million sermon illustrations years later. Dana's boss was named Joe, a crusty hardworking Christian man who was often short on patience but diligent on safety. Always before Dana could use a power tool, Joe gave safety instructions. Later in life when Dana owned his own power tools, he remembered the words of warning from Joe.

Joe said that many experienced carpenters are missing a finger or some portion of a finger. Some experienced carpenters have deep scars on their face. The reason, he said, is that experienced carpenters tend to get comfortable with power tools. They use them for so long, and know them so well, they disregard simple safety measures. These long time carpenters don't take the time to put the safety on the saw or wear goggles or gloves or protective gear—precautions that would take two seconds. And wham! There goes a finger lying in the sawdust. Joe said, "Dana, don't ever get comfortable with dangerous things. Not at work and not in your personal life."

In midlife we get comfortable with so many things. Maybe we just get restless, thinking there is something better out there. We begin to take things for granted: our spouse, our home, our blessings, our salvation, and our prayer life. We forget to put the safety down and by neglect we give sin an entrance into our lives. I would guess not many midlife failures are intentional. Most of them happen from our taking the mindset that we have this "spiritual stuff" mastered. Sin won't get me! I am too experienced to be tripped up. And before we know it—Wham!

A home, a marriage, a job, or something else we value, is lying in the sawdust.

Dear one, every day matters. Every action counts for something. Every word spoken has an effect. *"Watch over your heart with all diligence, for from it flows the springs of life"* (Proverbs 4:23). The safety for our hearts and our lives is our walk with the Lord. It is a daily renewing of our hearts and minds through His Word and through prayer. You and I can never get casual about meeting with God through Christ. At our daily altar, the Holy Spirit makes us aware of sin or possible sin in our lives. It is there that conviction and confession are nailed down. Our time with the Lord prompts us to remember all He has done for us, not only through the death and resurrection of Christ but also through the daily blessings, the needs met and the grace given. When we remember, we are filled with thanksgiving. Our personal time with the Lord is not a legalistic ritual, but rather a submission to any adjustment that needs to be made in our lives by Him. Let us all heed the warning to "put the safety down" and never get complacent about the things of God or about our daily walk with Him. It matters! It matters in all seasons of life! We never outgrow our need to walk closely with our Savior.

Rebekah did not just wake up one day and discover her home was a mess. The mess happened gradually, over time, until the consequences were overwhelming. The warning for us is while we walk closely with God we must also be diligent to guard our homes. Rebekah started with a loving marriage but ended with a relationship soured and filled with distrust. I don't ever want to be there. Nobody does.

Proverbs has so much to say about the home. Proverbs 14:1 speaks directly to the wife when it says, *"A wise woman builds her home but the foolish tears it down with her own hands."* If a woman wants to build her home wisely she must first build her marriage. Children can never overshadow the marriage relationship. To you young moms, that statement probably seems impossible.

One of my greatest regrets when I look back over my life is the season when my children were young. At times, I was a better mother than I was a wife. Children are so all-consuming. They will make you crazy sometimes. Moms feel the brunt of these crazy times, no matter if they stay at home or work outside of the home. A mother's heart as well as her time and energy, can easily be consumed by her children. At the end of the day there is nothing left for her husband.

Before some of you jump through the pages at me, let me say that Isaac was a bit of a pacifist, perhaps too laid back with his boys and certainly at fault on many levels. But Rebekah was strong-willed and tore at the fabric of her home, first by favoritism and then by deception. It seems the marriage ceased to be a priority when children came into the home. Ladies, guarding your marriage is a means of guarding your home. Make your spouse a priority even in the busy years. Find creative ways to glue your family together. But know, in the end, the greatest adhesive for the home and the greatest gift to your children is a healthy marriage.

Proverbs 24:1 says, *"Wisdom builds a house."* Oh, be wise with your homes, with your husbands, with your children. I get it. Marriage is not always easy and children are not always a delight. This is not a marriage manual or a child rearing book. There are many people much more qualified than I to give help in those areas. But I am here to wave the red flag of warning as we observe the life of Rebekah. Her life warns us that our walk with God matters in every season of life and urges us to guard our homes by first guarding our marriages.

Along with lessons to learn and warnings to heed, there is an admonition to hear. Anything in our lives that must be concealed or covered up will yield significant consequences. Let me say that another way. If there is anything about our behavior that must be kept a secret, that behavior will eventually harm us and the people we love. We are not meant to live secret lives. If there is any plan, any habit, any relationship, any circumstance about which you must lie or deceive in order to continue, rest assured, it is sinful. Let me be clear, I am not saying we have to hang all our dirty laundry out for the world to see or tell everything we know. This is not about discretion and discernment. This admonition is about secrecy with the intent to deceive.

Foremost, Rebekah stopped trusting God. She did not trust Him to bring about His own prophecy. She, like Sarah, tried to help God out. Go back and read how that turned out for Sarah. Rebekah, however, adds trouble to her lack of trust. She devises a plan to trick her husband and manipulate events. At least Sarah brought Abraham in on her plans. There was no duplicity involved for Sarah. But Rebekah chose deceit, which Webster's defines as causing someone to believe an untruth. She deceived Isaac and her home never recovered.

To me, there are few things more hurtful in a relationship than deception. It leaves one feeling used and certainly unloved. It destroys trust. It breeds suspicion and paranoia in a relationship. It will make a marriage ripe for ruin. Deception spawns an emptiness of soul in both the deceiver and the deceived that only the Lord Himself can fill and heal. Rebekah chose to weave a lie that would dupe her husband into blessing her favored son Jacob instead of the older son Esau. She chose to sacrifice her home in order to get her way. Of course Jacob was part of the trickery. He was a grown man and certainly knew it was wrong. But Rebekah takes the lead in this situation. She formulates the plan and her plan only feeds Jacob's bent toward deception. It would be a character flaw that would dog him for decades and God would finally have to cripple him to heal him.

Listen, listen, listen dear reader: you can choose your sin but you cannot choose the consequences. In choosing to deceive, Rebekah could not foresee the murderous rage of Esau, the broken heart of her husband or the loss of Jacob to a distant land. Sin always has unforeseen consequences. That is why Scripture is plain. God hates deception. Proverbs 6:16-19 lists seven things God hates. Haughty eyes and a lying tongue top the list. A person who sows discord ends the list. Rebekah covered the gamut. But we do not have to follow her example. In fact, we must not.

"Search me, O God, and know my heart," cries the psalmist. Can't I know my own heart? Can't we all discern our own motives and analyze our own thoughts? NO. Jeremiah 17:9 states, *"The heart is more deceitful than all else and is desperately sick; who can understand it?"* Our heart, our inner self, is clever enough to fool us. We can convince ourselves that our actions are justified, our motives are altruistic and our means justify the ends. That is why we need the spotlight of the Word and the Holy Spirit to investigate every aspect of our mind, emotions, motives, words and actions. Each day we must submit ourselves to the searchlight of the Lord. The writer of Hebrews likens the Word of God to an instrument which is sharper than a two-edged sword. It is sharp enough to cut like a

knowledgeable surgeon's scalpel. It slices through the soul and spirit and is able to judge between thoughts and motives. We cannot do this for ourselves.

Sin is subtle. It rarely makes a loud appearance in our lives. Instead it slithers in unnoticed and eventually makes a home. The Spirit of God and the Word of God are the tools used to dislodge sin. The Word of God exposes sin in our lives and the Holy Spirit gives us the wisdom and the power to deal with it according to Scripture. 1 John 1:9 tells us we are to confess our sins. Confession means agreeing with God. When we confess, we are not giving God new information. We simply agree with Him on what is sin. We acknowledge it verbally and we ask His forgiveness. He in turn is faithful and just, forgiving our sins and cleansing us from all unrighteousness. Confession and cleansing are meant to be part of our daily lives. For me, sometimes they are hourly!

The psalmist cries out for the Lord to search him, but he also asks the Lord to see if there is anything in his life that harms others. Sin is never a one man show. No matter how secretive, our sin always affects someone else. Many times it is those we love the most and those who are closest to us. Learn quickly from Rebekah. Do not give sin an opportunity to harm you or your walk with the Lord or the people you love. Live open, honest lives, connected daily with the Lord through His Word and time spent in prayer. Let Him search you daily for anything that might cause harm. Confess it immediately, turn from it, and thank Him for His cleansing. And live in confidence that you are a woman of grace

So was Rebekah a woman of grace? Yes. Even though Scripture never records any repentance. Even though she seems to have died bitter and joyless. Even though the consequences of her actions played out for decades. Rebekah is a woman of grace because God's grace is not limited by our actions.

Grace is always at work. Rebekah is still a chosen woman, chosen to be a part of God's great plan to create a people who would form a nation which would birth a Savior. She was chosen to be the wife of Isaac, the child of promise. She was chosen to bear twins, the younger of the two becoming Israel, the father of a nation. None of these things were by Rebekah's design. It was grace at work in history and in her personally. Any time sinful people have a relationship with Holy God; it is based on God's grace. Anytime God uses imperfect people to carry out His perfect plans, it is grace at work. Grace superseded Rebekah's sinful choices and her shortsighted decisions. When it comes to the sovereign plans of God, grace is always bigger than our choices.

Rebekah simply missed out on the joy of walking in grace. She missed the pleasure of communing with God and being in His presence. She bypassed the adventure of watching God work out His plan in Jacob's life. She laid down the peace of trusting God and instead picked up the slavery of works.

You may look at Rebekah's life and on some level identify with her. We all make shortsighted decisions. We all sin. We all take matters into our own hands at times and resist trusting the Lord. So how do we stop before the collateral damage is extensive?

We surrender.

Surrender is the difference between Sarah and Rebekah. Surrender is coming to the place where we take our hands off of everything and let the Lord have His way. We stop manipulating, deceiving, lying, managing, coercing and cajoling our lives, our circumstances and the lives of those we love. We abandon our will to the will of the Christ. We do this by responding to the work of the Holy Spirit in our lives. Paul tells us in Philippians 2:13, *"It is God at work in you, both to will (to want to) and to do His good pleasure."* Dear reader, God will put in your heart the desire to please Him as well the ability to please Him. We in turn trust Him and obey Him.

As the hymn implores, "Trust and obey for there's no other way to be happy in Jesus, but to trust and obey." That is the essence of surrender and surrender is the place of greatest joy and contentment for the believer. Surrender is where we find victory as well as peace. Surrendering to Christ is how we *finish strong*.

For Group Discussion

Read Genesis 24-28

1. Rebekah displays many admirable characteristics in the first half of her life. Which characteristics do you most admire in Rebekah? Are there any of her good qualities you would like strengthened in your own life?

2. Mid-life proved to be a negative turning point for Rebekah. How can we avoid the same mistake?

3. Family relationships can be challenging. How can we apply Proverbs 3:5-6 to any difficult relationship?

4. For Rebekah and Isaac, marriage seemed to take a back seat to children. Why did this become a detriment to their marriage and ultimately the family as a whole? What are some practical ways women can guard their marriage and ultimately their home?

   How does our personal walk with the Lord, or lack of it, affect others?

5. Read Psalm 19: 12-14, Psalm 26:2, and Psalm 139: 23-24. Discuss the meaning of these verses.

   How could Rebekah's life have been different had she applied these truths to her circumstances?

   Sometimes sin becomes so deeply embedded in our lives, we no longer recognize it as sin. How can the truth of these verses guard us from sin?

3

LEAH

(AND RACHEL)
Seeing Your Significance

I recently saw a Facebook post that caught my attention. It was a picture of two women, each one choking the other. Oddly, both women are smiling. The caption implied that only a person with a sister could understand the picture. The Facebook post is amusing for women like me who consider their sibling relationships a huge blessing. But for others, the post might not be so humorous. In Scripture, Leah and her younger sister Rachel seem to have each other in a choke hold. The problem is neither of them is smiling.

As we follow the genealogy of Christ in Matthew 1, Leah is the third woman in the lineage of Jesus. Like Sarah and

Rebekah, her name is not mentioned in the list of names but she is silently present as a wife of Jacob and the mother of Judah. It is difficult to study Leah without also taking notice of her sister, Rachel, who is also a wife of Jacob. Yes, life gets messy for these sisters.

When women are asked to identify themselves, most women will describe themselves in terms of relationships. They are someone's wife, daughter, mom, aunt, friend, employer or employee. Women usually see themselves as linked to other people. What a wonderful way to be identified, yet there is a danger in being solely identified by relationships that can change and fluctuate.

Even though they are sisters and they both marry Jacob, Leah and Rachel are very different women. Genesis 29 and 30 give us insight into their differences, their heartaches and their search for significance. It is a sad account of two women seeking acceptance and significance in places that provide neither. As we compare Leah and Rachel, there is much to learn about our own identity and our value as women of grace.

Characteristics of Leah and Rachel

Jacob is fleeing from his brother Esau. His mother Rebekah directs him east, toward the home of her brother Laban. As Genesis 29 begins, Jacob has journeyed far and finds himself at a well where sheep gather to drink water. He inquires of the local shepherds about Laban. Yes, they know him. In fact Laban's daughter Rachel is coming with sheep to this very well, at this very moment. The meeting of Jacob and Rachel is emotional and even romantic. She takes him home to her father Laban. There Jacob finds a place of rest and work, comfort and family.

Jacob has the reputation in Scripture of being a deceiver. It must run in the family because his Uncle Laban exhibits the same traits of deception. Laban is clever; he reels Jacob into employment using the one tender spot in Jacob's heart. Rachel. Jacob vows to work seven years, if in the end, his payment is the hand of Rachel in marriage. Laban agrees. To Jacob, seven years seems like a few days because of his great love for Rachel.

Those years of waiting had to be the most romantic, anticipatory years imaginable. The eyes that meet at mealtime. The hands that brush against each other in passing. The stolen kiss when watering sheep. The long walks at the end of the day. What a story! What a romance! But there is a problem. Her name is Leah, introduced in Scripture as the *older* sister of Rachel.

Most of us would never compare our children, especially our daughters, when it comes to physical beauty. But in this instance, the Bible draws a contrast between Rachel and Leah. Rachel is beautiful of form and face. She has a face and a figure that catches a man's eye and holds him until he is smitten. She is what movie stars are made of. Crazy beautiful. Leah on the other hand is rather plain. In fact the Bible says she has weak eyes. Many scholars have tried to define that ancient term but whichever way you slice it, she can't hold a candle to her younger sister's beauty. Maybe Leah has a great personality. Maybe she can sew and cook and work like a horse. But Scripture lets us know she is not attractive and Jacob only has eyes for Rachel.

That's not fair! Physical beauty is not the standard by which we judge people, right? But so often we do. And if we are not careful we will judge and value ourselves by someone's definition of physical attractiveness. It is problematic, but most people are naturally drawn to physical beauty. If Rachel and Leah were presented to us today and we were asked which one would be God's choice for the lineage of Christ, many of us would pick Rachel, simply based on her looks. But thankfully, we are not God. God chooses the least likely. Scripture shows a contrast in physical appearance, loudly proclaiming God's plans are based on grace, not human standards.

Jacob works seven years and now the time has come to be paid. It is time to marry his beloved Rachel. Laban however, has different plans. Ancient culture requires a father to marry off the oldest daughter before any of her younger sisters can marry. I don't know why that little bit of information did not come up for discussion in those first seven years. Maybe because Laban thinks no man would ever want weak eyed Leah—at least not a man of Laban's choosing. In Laban's mind, the only way to get Leah a husband is to trick the poor guy into marrying her. And so Jacob, the deceiver, is deceived.

I have often wondered how Laban pulled off this deception. How did he substitute Leah for Rachel and still get Jacob to say "I do"? Perhaps there was much wine coupled with heavy Middle Eastern veils over the bride as well as the dim light of an evening wedding. Somehow Laban (and Leah) pulled it off. The morning after the wedding night, Jacob discovers his bride is not his beloved Rachel but her older sister, Leah. Unfortunately, the deal is sealed. He said "I do". He slept with her. Jacob is outraged. I can't blame him.

In a dubious effort to correct the wrong, crafty Laban proposes a solution. If Jacob will complete the customary wedding week with Leah, then Jacob can also acquire Rachel as a second wife. The price for Rachel will be Jacob's service to Laban for seven more years. Jacob agrees. At the end of his honeymoon week with Leah, Jacob marries Rachel. Imagine. In one week, Laban marries off both daughters and gains a hard working son-in-law for another seven years. In the same week, Jacob gains two wives, seven more years of employment and a boatload of troubles. Laban definitely got the better deal.

Polygamy was never God's intention for marriage. It is presented in Scripture as man's actions but not God's plan. Later in Scripture, multiple wives are permitted only for kings and eventually not permitted at all. Wherever polygamy appears in the Bible, trouble is also present. A man cannot live peaceably with two wives, and certainly not when the wives are also sisters. The contrast between the two women continues as the truth is revealed: *"And Jacob loved Rachel more than Leah."*

You and I will never understand the mercy of God or His ways. Genesis 29:31 is filled with mercy and mystery. Seeing that Leah is unloved, God blesses her with children by her husband Jacob. Rachel, on the other hand, is loved by Jacob but remains childless. A rivalry which had probably festered for years now erupts between the sisters.

In the closing verses of Genesis 29, Leah has three sons. With each birth she dreams of gaining her husband's love and not just the duty of his body. Each time she is disappointed. She has Jacob's children, but she will never have his heart. With the birth of her fourth son, Judah, Leah chooses to praise the Lord instead of clamoring for Jacob's affection. In light of her momentary refocus, it is interesting that God chooses Judah to be the heir of the promise. According to Matthew 1, Judah is the next step on the road to hope.

Before we feel too much sympathy for unloved Leah, remember she was part of Laban's deception. She knew what she was doing. No one had to drag Leah kicking and screaming to Jacob's marriage bed. She deceived both Jacob and Rachel and neither her husband nor her sister ever forgot it.

Rachel, the beautiful and the loved, watches her older sister bless Jacob with children. Rachel becomes jealous. Even though she has Jacob's heart, she cannot have his children. She blames her husband for her misery and sets into motion a dizzying account of two wives, two female slaves, a house full of Jacob's children and the very definition of dysfunctional.

Rachel gives her slave, Bilhah, to Jacob in order to have children by the slave. The children of Bilhah, fathered by Jacob, are considered the children of Rachel. It is the same custom that drove Sarah to give Hagar to Abraham. Meanwhile, Leah has stopped bearing children and follows Rachel's example. Leah gives her slave to Jacob in order to claim more children. Jacob obliges both wives and four more sons are born for his wives through their female slaves. I often wonder if Jacob is enjoying the assortment of women or if he is just trying to hang on, hoping for peace at the end of the day. These sisters are wrestling with each other and producing a home filled with discord and jealousy.

When the riveting account of Chapter 30 concludes, Jacob has eleven sons and a daughter. Rachel has finally conceived and given birth to Joseph. While Joseph is not the son God would choose to be in the direct lineage to Christ, he is the son that would later save his entire family. Jacob's dysfunctional family will become a nation and one day birth a Savior. God gives Rachel one more son before she dies, demonstrating again that grace prevails, even in the jealousy and drama of Jacob's household.

Do you see it? Each woman wanted what the other had. One wanted Jacob's heart. One wanted Jacob's children. Each sister thought she would have peace of mind, peace of heart, acceptance and significance if only she had what her sister had. Instead of peace, there is chaos.

Sometimes we are like Rachel and Leah, searching for something no man, no child, no job, and no physical beauty can give us. We, like Rachel and Leah, are creating havoc and living in the consequences, all the while, longing for the emptiness in our lives to be filled. We vie for the wrong things. We seek acceptance where it will never be found. We look around at everyone else's life and feel we have been shortchanged. We have forgotten the words of Psalm 16:11, *"In Thy presence is fullness of joy."* Is there any rest from our futile search for significance?

Rest only comes in knowing Christ. If you are a child of God, having a relationship with Him through Jesus Christ, your identity and your significance comes through knowing Christ. Your value as a person does not fluctuate based on earthly relationships or circumstances. Your worth to God is not diminished by your past baggage nor is it increased by your daily accomplishments. You are significant because Christ lives in you.

Who Am I in Christ?

Early Christians needed to know the same things we need to know. They needed to understand their identity in Christ. They needed to be assured that God's evaluation of worth is different than society's. In his letter to the church at Ephesus, the Apostle Paul reminds these new Christians of their identity

63

in Christ and all that is available to them in Christ. The first three chapters of Ephesians read almost like a laundry list, listing and explaining all that we have and all that we are. Yet Paul is so clear, it is ours because of grace, the grace of God made available to us through Jesus Christ.

The world's standards have changed very little since ancient times. The world tells us we are significant because of our physical appearance. It tells us we must have the right education or pedigree. Society dictates our significance by how well our children perform or how influential our husbands are. It deceives us into evaluating ourselves based on our paycheck or our occupation. But at the end of the day, each standard of significance the world uses can change, crumble or die. Our identity, our significance, and our value as women must be found in the unchangeable person of Christ.

Who are you in Christ? What is your value to God? Using the first chapters of Ephesians, let's explore five words; all beginning with the letter **S**. Each word will help us discern our significance.

You are <u>sought</u>.

God came after you. He pursued you, not to harm you but rather to have a loving relationship with you. The entire Bible is the story of God pursuing sinful people. We do not seek God. He seeks us. Ephesians 1:4 says, *"He chose us in Him (Jesus) before the foundations of the world."* I can't fully understand that concept but it is repeated throughout Scripture. God chose me and you. He chose us before we ever knew we needed Him.

As a single gal, I liked being pursued. Call me old fashioned but I like it when, even today, my husband pursues me. I like it when he takes the lead and plans events, or brings flowers or starts the conversation. I enjoyed the dating phase of our lives when he wrote letters and said tender words that made my heart swoon. I liked knowing, then and now, my man only has eyes for me. Young love or old love, it feels good to be pursued.

Now translate that pursuit to the God of the universe. The one who created heaven and earth. The one who carved out oceans and seas and mountains and valleys. The God who flung the stars into space and designed the DNA of every living creature. This God thrills in pursuing you. He delights in His greatest creation—you! He wants you to know Him as the lover of your soul. He calls out to you like the groom calls out to his bride in Song of Solomon. He invites you into a divine love relationship that will never wane, or change or die.

Scripture is clear; God seeks us while we are sinners. He loves us when we are imperfect. Romans 5:8 states that God demonstrated His love toward us while we were still sinners. His pursuit of us does not wait until we are good enough, clean enough, pretty enough, wealthy enough, or educated enough. The loving Heavenly Father chooses to come looking for imperfect people—like us.

I cannot explain all that Scripture means in the use of the word *chosen*. Theologians have debated it for centuries. But the word is there. It is never presented in negative terms as to say some are chosen and some are not. Spiros Zodhiates writes, "No one who is saved can say that he is saved because of his own choice. His salvation is in response to God's choice of him. And, on the other hand, no one who is lost can say that he is lost because God willed him to be lost." [2]

Coupled with the word *chosen* is the word *predestined*. These words are used together in Romans 8:29-30 and

Ephesians 1:4-5. If you want to make a lot of religious people nervous, just say the word *predestined*. Denominations argue over it—well—religiously. It means *predetermined*. Like the word *chosen*, it is never used in negative terms. The Bible does not say some are predestined to heaven and others predestined to hell. In fact, predestined is only used to describe the purpose or status of a person and not their eternal destination. Paul writes in Ephesians 1:5 that we as believers are predestined to adoption as sons. Adoption is our status not our eternal destination. Paul is not using the word *predestined* to confuse us but rather to affirm us.

In ancient Rome, an adopted child could never be disowned. Furthermore, that adopted child has the all rights and privileges of the family. As an adult, the adopted child not only has everything but can also use everything made available to him by the father. This is exciting news for us as believers.

Scripture says God predetermined, or decided beforehand, that when we come into His family by spiritual birth (John 3:3), we have the status of an adult adopted child. Our status as an adopted child means we can never be disowned. In addition, we are immediately blessed with **every** spiritual blessing in Christ Jesus (Ephesians 1:3). That means we got all of Jesus we are ever going to get. We do not come into the family of God and get Jesus in increments. The journey of the Christian is not to get more of Jesus. The journey of the Christian is learning to live fully in what we already have. And with adult adopted status—we have it all in Christ, never to be disowned.

What a pursuit! What a blessing! Do you see your value and your significance to Father God? Dear woman, God sought you. He came looking for you. He has called you into a relationship with Him. In Christ you have everything the Father has to offer. He will never reject you or turn you away. And He does it all because He loves you. He shows that love through His grace; grace that comes to us at great cost to God.

You are <u>saved</u>.

I grew up in a Baptist church so all of my life I have heard the word *saved*. It has been part of my vernacular for so long, I sometimes take for granted the depth of its meaning. Paul uses a different word in Ephesians 1:7, the word *redemption*. We can put it under the same heading as *saved* but there is tenderness and fullness in the word *redemption* that we would do well to explore.

*In Him, we have redemption through His blood, the forgiveness of our trespasses, according to the riches of His grace (*Ephesians 1:7).

In the original Greek, the root word *redeem* means *to buy back by paying the full price*. The ancient readers of Ephesians would understand the concept of redemption since slavery was a part of their culture and people could be bought and sold like cattle. Scripture is teaching we are bought by God, the price of our redemption being the blood of Jesus. There is a lot of theology in that simple verse. Bought from whom? Bought by blood?

We come into this world as sinners. We do not become sinners when we commit acts of sin. We commit acts of sin because we are already sinners, born with the sinful nature of Adam (Romans 5-8). Simply put, all have sinned because all are sinners (Romans 3:23). Without Christ, we are spiritually dead and our lives are enslaved to sin by our sinful nature, the sinful world system and the Devil (Ephesians 2:1-2). Indeed we are created by God but because of sin we are enslaved with no hope of freeing ourselves.

Grace intervenes.

But God *being rich in mercy, because of His great love with which He loved us, even when we were dead in our transgressions, made us alive together with Christ (by grace you have been saved)* (Ephesians 2:4).

God steps into the hopelessness of slavery to sin and pays the full price to set us free. The Old Testament lays the foundation for blood as a sacrifice for sin. A lamb was offered to cover the sins of the people. Life is in the blood and life must be sacrificed as payment for sin (Leviticus 17:11 and Romans 6:23). The Old Testament is a foreshadowing of the New Testament, everything in the Old pointing us to Jesus. The full price for our sin is not the blood of a goat or lamb but the precious, unblemished, sinless blood of Christ (1 Peter 1:18-19).

Do you see your value? Do you see your worth? God has paid the supreme price to buy you out of sin's slavery. He has lavished forgiveness and grace on you. He has made you His own. You are saved. You are redeemed. You are a recipient of His grace.

My daddy used to tell a story about a boy and a boat. It is a sermon illustration he used fifty years ago but it still impacts me today. Perhaps a hundred other preachers have told the same story but I can only credit my dad with its telling.

A little boy crafted a toy boat. He took great care in carving the wood for the small hull. He cut out a perfectly proportioned sail and tied it to the handmade mast. He painted the boat and named it, "Especially Mine."

The little boy wanted to try out his creation, so he went down to the river and set his precious boat afloat. A cruel wind grabbed the sail and the current carried the boat out of the reach of the little boy. The waves beat it and pushed the boat further and further downstream. The little boat was lost and the boy was heartbroken.

Several days later while walking down the street, the boy looked into the window of the local toy store. There on display was his toy boat. He knew it was his boat. He had crafted every piece of it and there was the name, "Especially mine" still painted on the side. He rushed into the store brimming with excitement! "Mister, mister, that is my toy boat in your window. It's mine. I made it. I want it back!"

The owner of the toy store was not persuaded. He told the young boy that the boat had been found and now it was for sale. If the boy wanted the boat, he would have to purchase it. Undaunted, the boy left the store and began to sell everything he had. He brought all the money he had acquired to the toy store and laid it on the counter as payment for the boat he had made.

The boy left the toy store that day with his creation back in his hands. His boat was his again. The boy held that little boat and joyfully exclaimed, "Little boat, you are mine, you are mine, you are twice mine! I made you and I bought you. You are mine!"

I can still hear the teardrop in my dad's voice as he tells the story, knowing full well the price God paid to redeem us. Dear reader, you are created by God. He crafted every part of you yet sin took you captive. But God, in His rich mercy and grace, gave all that He had to buy you back. He has written "Especially Mine" across your heart. You are redeemed. You are forgiven. You are valued. Rejoice.

You are <u>sealed</u>.

Recently, I mailed a package to my son. I sealed it to keep the contents safe and dry and clean as it traveled across four states through the postal service to my son's doorstep. The package arrived intact, the seal unbroken and the contents secure. In a similar way, our salvation is sealed.

Jesus says in John 10:28, no one is able to snatch us out of the Father's hand. We are secure. Remember our status? We cannot be disowned and our salvation cannot be stolen from us. Paul uses the picture of a seal in Ephesians 1:13b-14a to teach us about our security in Christ. He writes, *"You were sealed in Him with the Holy Spirit of promise, who is given as a pledge of our inheritance."*

In ancient times, a letter or document was sealed by the sender. The sender had his own unique seal, usually a ring or some kind of signet. Melted wax held the document closed and the sender pressed his seal into the hot wax. The process of sealing indicated the authenticity and ownership of the document. An unbroken seal assured the recipient of the letter's security. A seal was also used in ancient times to represent a signature in a completed transaction or agreement.

The Holy Spirit is God's seal on our salvation. Along with every spiritual blessing, we are blessed with the Holy Spirit the moment we come into the family of God. Like the indention from the ancient signet ring, the presence of the Holy Spirit in our lives indicates we belong to God, Jesus is our Lord and our salvation is secure. The Holy Spirit is the unique Spirit of the Lord Jesus Christ living within each believer, marking us as His and authenticating our relationship with Him.

The Spirit, like the ancient seal, also indicates a finished transaction. We have once and for all been transferred out of the kingdom of darkness and into the kingdom of Light (Colossians 1:13). The deed to our lives has been signed with the blood of Christ and sealed with the Holy Spirit. God cannot and will not break His promises to us. He will not let us go. The Spirit in us is the guarantee.

The Holy Spirit is also described as a pledge. A pledge is a promise of something yet to come. If you buy a house, you put down earnest money as a pledge that the rest will be paid. Likewise, an engagement ring is a pledge of betrothal at some point in the future. When the Bible describes the Holy Spirit as the pledge of our inheritance, it means we are guaranteed something in the future. Our guarantee for the future is Heaven and the presence of the Holy Spirit in our lives is the pledge that someday we will indeed live there.

Are you catching a glimpse of your value to God? We belong to Him. He has sought us and saved us and sealed us. We can rest from the futile struggle of seeking worldly significance as we better understand how valuable, how priceless we are to the Father. Yet there is even more.

You are <u>seated</u>.

My parents hosted many guests in our home when I was growing up. We often shared a meal with traveling missionaries or visiting ministers. My mother always prepared wonderful food but she never served the food in a casual buffet style. She never said, "Just grab a plate, help yourself and sit anywhere you want." Instead, the table was perfectly set and each person was assigned a particular place to sit. My father sat at the head of the table. Our guest was seated to the right of my father, which was deemed a place of honor. I don't know if the seating arrangement was an etiquette thing or a spiritual thing. But it was definitely my mother's thing and I think of our dinner table when I read Ephesians 2:6, *"...and seated us with Him in the heavenly places."*

Jesus is seated at the right hand of the Father (Hebrews 5:1, Mark14:62, Mark 16:19). The right hand of God is always viewed in Scripture as a place of honor, authority and power. Jesus is the only one who occupies this place, yet Ephesians says we are seated with Jesus. There is a wealth of doctrine in that simple statement of Ephesians 2:6. But in the most simplistic terms, when God looks at us, Jesus says, "She's with me."

Spiritually, we are seated at the head table, beside the guest of honor. We are privileged to sit at His table not as beggars and sinners but as redeemed family members who are heirs of God and joint heirs with Christ (Romans 8:17). It is a place of honor but also humility as we recognize we are not seated because of our own merit. It is Christ alone who gives us access to the Table of God. I am amazed and humbled that He would raise me up and seat me beside Christ. Oh, how He loves us. Oh, how He values us. Soak it in dear woman. The world's applause and esteem pales in the light of this truth.... we are seated with Christ in the heavenly places.

You are <u>strengthened</u>.

It is great to know we are sought, saved, sealed and seated but hey—we have to live in the real world. We have real jobs, real families and real problems. How do all of these spiritual blessings play out in real life situations?

Paul prays two prayers in Ephesians. The first prayer is in Ephesians 1:18 ff. He prays that the eyes of our hearts will be enlightened, understanding all that is available to us in Christ. His second prayer is recorded in Ephesians 3:14-21. This second prayer is for our ability to practice daily our position in Christ. In his prayer, Paul presents the "recipe" for living out our spiritual blessings in real life situations. The primary ingredient is power.

"...that He would grant you, according to the riches of His glory, to be strengthened with power through His Spirit in the inner man: so that Christ may dwell in your hearts by faith, and that you, being rooted and grounded in love, may be able to comprehend with all the saints what is the breadth and length and height and depths, and to know the love of Christ which surpasses knowledge, that you may be filled up to all the fullness of God" (Ephesians 3:16-19).

We can live the Christian life because we are strengthened with power. This power is not physical strength but spiritual strength. We are able to be and do everything God desires because we are empowered by the Holy Spirit of Christ who lives in us. He does not work from the outside in, modifying our behavior with external rewards. Neither does He change our circumstances, making them pleasant so it is easier to live victoriously. He works from the inside out, changing us on the inside, in the inner man.

The purpose of power is threefold. First, we are strengthened with power so that Christ may dwell in our hearts by faith. *To dwell* means to settle down and be at home. It means we give Him access to every part of our lives which includes our mind, our attitudes, our habits, our emotions, our actions, and our words.

I am not the greatest house keeper in the world but I give the appearance that I am. I clean the rooms other people will see. The living room is usually spotless and gives a good first impression. The kitchen and the family room are never perfect but the casual clutter is palatable. However, if an unexpected guest arrives, I shut the bedroom door, seal off the laundry room and silently pray no one needs a bathroom. And certainly I would never invite a guest to peek into my disorganized closets, look under my beds or riffle through my pantry. There is dirt, dust and bedlam in all of the "off limits" places.

Likewise as Christians, we become accustomed to making good impressions. The visible areas of our lives are fairly well maintained and respectably clean. But Jesus wants to dwell in every part of us. To do this, we must give Him the keys to anything we have locked away from public viewing. We must invite Him into the places that are not clean and presentable. We must allow Him access to the habits no one knows about, the thoughts no one can see, the attitudes that creep into our lives, and the secret sins hidden from view.

As we give Christ access, the Holy Spirit uses the Word of God to clean out the hidden rooms of our lives. He lovingly convicts us and leads us to repentance. The Spirit also uses Scripture to teach us what is right and pure and good for our lives and then He enables us to implement it. Our response to His housecleaning is daily surrender and daily obedience.

It may seem like a scary thing to expose our hidden messes to the Lord, but understanding His great love for us eases our fears. Knowledge of His love is the second reason we are strengthened with power. The knowledge Paul refers to in Ephesians 3:19, is not head knowledge. It is experiential knowledge. We know the love of Christ because we have experienced it first hand in our lives. We have experienced His love through forgiveness, blessings and intervention in our daily lives. The love of Christ constrains us to obedience. It calls us to the highest plane of living. His love for us binds our hearts to His. We are not compelled to live for Christ out of duty but rather out of thanksgiving for His tender love toward us. The Holy Spirit living within us, bearing witness with the Word of God, constantly reminds us of God's great love for us.

Finally, when Christ dwells in every corner of our lives and we comprehend His great love for us, we will overflow with the fullness of God. We are not overflowing with the fullness of God because we got more of Jesus. We overflow because Jesus got more of us! The Holy Spirit has cleaned out all the dusty, dirty corners. He has exposed the sealed off places and tossed out the unwanted trash. He has occupied all the rooms of our heart and made us keenly aware of His great love for us. Every part of our lives is filled up with Christ and we overflow onto everyone around us.

Woman of grace, are you beginning to understand your great value to God and your significance in Christ? In contrast, Leah was looking for worth in things that could not give her lasting fulfillment. She wanted marriage to Jacob and bearing his children to be her banner of significance. Temporal things and earthly relationships cannot bear up under such weight.

They are destined to disappoint us eventually. ***But God***, in His great love and mercy, took Leah's shortsighted desires and covered them with grace. He blessed her with Judah, the lion from whom the scepter would never depart (Genesis 49:9-10). God gave her, by grace, a place in the lineage of the Savior and marked her forever as a woman of great worth. Whether or not she ever understood her value to God, we will never know.

But you dear reader, can soak in the goodness of God's amazing grace towards you. You can allow the truth to seep into your heart; the truth that God loved you enough to pursue you and choose you. He has made you part of His family, never to be disowned or abandoned. He has given you every spiritual blessing as your inheritance here on earth and He has promised Heaven as your inheritance in the future. He has placed the seal of the Holy Spirit on your life and seated you in a place of honor. Dear woman, God is working daily to strengthen you with power so that Jesus fills every corner of your life. His strength will give you confidence to walk in His love, overflowing as a testimony of His grace.

This is your identity. This is your value. This is your significance. You are a woman of grace, highly favored and richly blessed. Rejoice!

Questions for Discussion

Read Genesis 29:1 through 30:24. Read Ephesians 1:3 through 2:9 and Ephesians 3:16-19.

1. Leah went along with her father's deception to marry Jacob. What does this tell us about Leah?

   Rachel is beautiful and Jacob adores her but she is jealous of Leah. What does Rachel's jealousy tell us about her?

   Each woman struggled with her significance and her identity. Can you relate to their struggle in any way?

2. What is the danger of basing our identity solely on our relationships with others? For example: wife of, mother of, daughter of, sister of...

   Why is it futile to evaluate ourselves by society's standards?

3. What does it mean to be chosen by God? How does that make you feel?

4. Based on John 3:3 we come into the family of God by new birth or being born again. Our status in God's family, however, is that of an adult adopted child. What are the benefits of our status?

5. Explain what it means to be saved or redeemed? How does the experience of being bought back change the way we view ourselves?

6. We live in a real world with real problems. So why is it important that we are strengthened with power by the Spirit?

Christ wants to dwell, settle down and live, in every area of our lives. Read Psalm 139: 23-24 and Psalm 26:2. Apply these verses to the housecleaning the Lord wants to do in our lives.

4

TAMAR
Forgiving the Unforgivable

Tamar. Have you heard of her? Her story covers only one chapter in Genesis and it is not a Bible story we would tell to children. In fact, hers is one of the most distasteful and unseemly accounts in all of Scripture. And yet, her name is in the genealogy of Christ as recorded in Matthew. She is the first of five women whose names appear in the list, but she is not an Israelite. She is a Canaanite who got mixed up with Judah, the fourth son of Leah and the heir to the promise. Her story poses moral dilemmas for us, dilemmas that Scripture neither answers nor explains. The injustices of her story could leave us feeling hopeless if not for the resounding truth—

Grace Prevails.

Tamar's Story

Judah leaves his father's household and goes out to live among the pagan Canaanites. In the previous chapter of Genesis, he helped sell his younger brother Joseph into slavery, and then deceived his father saying Joseph was killed by a wild animal. Judah watched his father, Jacob, wither with inconsolable grief. Perhaps in an effort to escape his own guilt, Judah went to live with people who did not know God.

The Bible says Judah married a Canaanite woman who bore him three sons. The firstborn is named Er, the second is Onan and the youngest is Shelah. When Er is old enough to marry, Judah finds a wife for him among the pagan Canaanites. Her name is Tamar.

The events of Genesis 38 have few cultural parallels for us. Imposing our modern mindset onto this story will not help us make sense of it. Ancient customs and laws are in play throughout this account. For us it is uncommon for a father to choose a bride for his son. But for this ancient culture it is customary for Judah to choose the wife for his oldest son. Additionally, when Judah brings Tamar into his household, his family assumes responsibility for her for the rest of her life. There is no government program, no retirement account and no inheritance for a woman of that time. Tamar leaves the security of her own father's household and she becomes the wife of Er. Ultimately she is the responsibility of Judah because he is the patriarch of the family.

My heart goes out to this young woman. Her life is being dictated by someone else's decisions. Her father gives her to Judah. Judah gives her to Er. She has no say in the matter and unfortunately for Tamar, Er is wicked. In fact, he is so wicked, God kills him. That truth sucks the breath out of me every time I read it (Genesis 38:7). No details, no commentary, no specifics other than Er was wicked and the Lord said *enough*. Scripture neither apologizes for God's actions nor explains them. Holy God is at work. His authority stands whether we understand it or agree with it.

Because Er is described as wicked, my sanctified imagination wanders to Tamar. How wicked was he to her? What kind of abuse did she endure at his hands? What harsh words or ridicule did she bow beneath? What anger did her soft skin absorb? Even more disturbing, how often did Judah silently stand by and do nothing? I have to believe that judgment for Er was mercy for Tamar.

Mercy seems short-lived when Judah, the patriarch, gives Tamar to his second son, Onan. Deuteronomy 25:5-6 sheds light on this ancient practice called "levirate marriage". The second brother marries the widow of the first brother in order to produce children in the name of the dead brother. Thus the dead brother's place in the family is not lost and the dead brother is remembered. In addition, the first child born to the widow and the second brother is considered the firstborn child of the dead brother. This firstborn child is the primary heir to the patriarch's estate. (See what I mean? We have no cultural parallels.)

Onan marries Tamar. His responsibility is to produce children with her in the name of his dead brother. Onan refuses his responsibility. His refusal brings humiliation to Tamar. During each sexual encounter with her, Onan interrupts their intimacy and spills his seed on the ground. It is a display of contempt for his dead brother and his father's household. It is a display of rejection for Tamar. Judah, again, stands by silently. But God acts. He kills Onan.

We cannot begin to understand the ways of Holy God. So far, God may seem ruthless and reactionary in this story but two important truths stand out. First, sin is serious to God. He will not tolerate sin nor will He allow it to thwart His plans. The second truth we cannot fail to see is the merciful eye of God on Tamar. Er probably abused her. Onan rejected her. Judah ignored her. But God did not turn a blind eye. He chose her, simply by grace, to be in the lineage of Christ and pen her name in that list of broken lives that lead to hope. For Tamar, the road to hope is beset with injustice but grace will walk with her even when she is unaware.

Judah has lost two sons, both while married to Tamar. He is so out of touch with God, he assumes their deaths are Tamar's fault. He is reluctant to give his third son to her in marriage although that would be the progression under levirate law. Instead, he gives the excuse that Shelah is too young to marry. Therefore Tamar must go home to her father's house and wait until the youngest son is of age.

To us this may sound reasonable, but in the ancient culture it is almost criminal. Judah has shamed Tamar completely by sending her out of his household and back to her father. Legally, she should have been allowed to stay in Judah's home until it was time to marry Shelah. Her rejection by Judah will result in rejection by her own father. The perceived shame will cause her own father to regard her as a slave instead of a daughter. Judah has abdicated his responsibility for Tamar and in doing so, left her indigent. She has no husband or children to care and provide for her. She has no possessions. She has no safe place in the home of her birth. She leaves Judah's home with no future and no hope.

The years pass, and Tamar realizes that Judah has not only rejected her, he has also deceived her. He never intended to send for her when Shelah was grown. He did not want to lose another son to the woman. After all, the other two died while married to her. Judah's fear coupled with his lack of character, leave Tamar in dire straits. She must find a way back into her father-in-law's family. Legally, no one else can marry her. No one else can or will ever claim her. She has a rightful place inside Judah's family but outside of it, Tamar has nothing.

Judah's wife dies and lonely Judah decides to visit a nearby Canaanite city to have his flock of sheep sheared. He and his pagan friend Hirah will make the trip together. Tamar gets the news that her father-in-law will be passing by her home town on his way to Timnah. Desperate Tamar, who has nothing to lose, devises a plan. She will disguise herself as a pagan temple prostitute and seduce her father-in-law. If a child is conceived, she has a future in the house of Judah.

Temple prostitutes were common among the Canaanites. The women were paid for their sexual favors and the sexual act itself was considered worship to a pagan god. Judah could appease his loneliness and be in the good graces of pagan religion at the same time. It would not be difficult to deceive him and Tamar knew it.

She throws off her widow garments and puts on the veils of a prostitute and sits beside the road waiting for Judah. He sees her as he passes, never knowing it is his daughter-in-law. He is intrigued that a prostitute is on the roadside and not in the hustle and bustle of the city. He can, perhaps, enjoy her favors without the scrutiny of so many others. After all, he is lonely, she is available, so why not?

Tamar agrees to a tryst with Judah but asks for payment in advance. Judah promises to give her a goat from his flock when he returns from Timnah. She has thought this plan through and she is counting on Judah's lack of character as well as his sexual need. She asks for a pledge, a down payment, before she will please him. Eager to have his needs met and impatient with the bargaining of a prostitute, Judah gives her his seal (a signet ring), his belt and his staff. This is tantamount to giving up his driver's license, his social security card and his passport! He gave her every piece of identification he owned, assuming he could recover them later. What was he thinking, giving valuable items to a roadside prostitute? Obviously, sexual desire trumped common sense.

Once again the Bible is understated, giving us few emotional details. Tamar and Judah have a one-time sexual encounter. She conceives a child and goes home to wait for all hell to break loose. Three months later, it does.

When Judah leaves Timnah, he sends his friend Hirah back to the spot in the road where the prostitute sat. Hirah is to pay the prostitute with a goat and retrieve Judah's belongings. Unfortunately, the prostitute has disappeared and locals tell Hirah no temple prostitute has ever occupied that area of the road. Judah senses he has been duped. Guilty, angry and disgusted, Judah shrugs off the whole affair and justifies his behavior by his attempt to pay her. Oh well, who cares? She's just a whore. He returns to life as usual, trying to forget the whole unsavory incident.... until he gets the news his daughter-in-law Tamar, is pregnant.

Judah rages! He demands she be dragged from her father's house and burned alive. She is guilty of harlotry! The child she carries is an illegitimate child of harlotry. Both mother and unborn child must be destroyed!

Why all the rage and concern? Judah did not want her. He did not want her to marry his third son. He did not even want her in his tent. So why does he care so much about what she has done and who she has slept with and the child she is carrying? It all goes back to ancient laws and customs.

Even though Judah has disregarded Tamar, legally and morally she is still married to Judah's family. She is the still considered the widow of the first son. The first child she bears will be the legal heir to Judah's estate. Even an illegitimate child. Certainly Judah's anger is a double standard. Judah could have as many sexual exploits as he wished, strewing illegitimate children all over the countryside. But because of her marriage to firstborn Er, Tamar is linked to Judah's household forever. Her first child gets it all—Judah's wealth, Judah's name, Judah's legacy. This child is Tamar's ticket to hope. This child would be her future. Judah would see to it that Tamar had neither. To Judah, her pregnancy is an offense that must be rectified by death. He has no idea the child she carries is his.

It must have been a terrifying scene for Tamar. The servants of Judah drag Tamar kicking and screaming from her father's house, without a word of protest from her family. Judah's men stand with torches burning, ready to sever once and for all Judah's ties with this troublesome woman. Every man in her life has hurt her, abused her, rejected her or neglected her. Now she would be extinguished like a pesky insect and not even a whimper of sorrow would be breathed by any man who has ever known her.

Tamar, however, will have the last word. In the chaos of events, she produces Judah's signet ring, belt and staff. She proclaims the child in her womb belongs to the owner of these items. There is no doubt. Judah is the father. Tamar's life is spared.

I hope God has a replay button in heaven. I would like to see this scene for myself. I want to see the shock and disbelief on those men's faces. I want to hear the silence that hangs in the air as they all try to comprehend what has just happened. I want to see Tamar shoulders sag with relief, knowing there is hope for her and her unborn child.

When Judah gets the news, he recalls the roadside tryst with a temple prostitute. The pieces come together in his mind. He ascertains what has happened and he hangs his head in defeat. He makes a declaration in Genesis 38:26 which sounds like repentance. He knows he has been wrong in his treatment of Tamar. He admits she is more righteous than he in that her actions were a desperate attempt to force the blessings which he had denied her.

The Bible says Judah never had any sexual relationship with her again. That statement indicates Tamar came back into Judah's household and lived like a family member. There is no record she ever marries Judah's youngest son. She does not need to. A child has been produced to continue the family name, as well as remember the oldest son, inherit the wealth of Judah, and care for Tamar in her old age. In fact, twin sons are born to Tamar. The first twin is Perez and he is the child that will carry on the lineage of Christ.

The Bible gives no moral commentary on the actions of Tamar. It does not point out her sin or label her as evil even though she deceived her father-in-law and had an incestuous relationship with him. Likewise, Judah's actions are neither explained nor moralized even though we can read in Genesis he was sinful long before his dealings with Tamar (Genesis 37:26ff). Er and Onan are the only people in this account who are deemed evil and God deals with them swiftly. This entire story is not included in Scripture to primarily teach us lessons in morality. It is included to show us God's grace.

Without the covering of God's grace, this is just another twisted account of abuse, neglect, deception, incest and heartache. But Tamar is a woman of grace. God chooses her, a pagan Canaanite, to be in the family of Judah and ultimately in the lineage of Christ. God mercifully protects her from evil husbands. Even in her desperate and immoral plan, He blesses her with two sons and brings her back into the house of Judah. Through a series of grace filled events, Judah, his ten bothers, his father Jacob and all of their families move to Egypt to escape famine (Genesis 42-47). Tamar and her sons are with them(Genesis 46:12). She is not only a part of Judah's family but also his extended family, which becomes the nation of Israel. Certainly, as a part of this family, Tamar comes to know the God of Israel. She watches her father-in-law, Judah, reconcile with his brother Joseph (Genesis 46-47). She hears Grandfather Jacob bless Judah as the lion from whom the scepter shall never depart (Genesis 49:9-10). She knows she is a part of God's plan. Nothing she has done in the past and nothing in the past that has been done to her can thwart God's plan or divert His grace. His grace is bigger than her past and it is greater than her hurts and her choices.

It may seem like there are few life lessons for us to take away from this ancient account of Tamar. Yet all of us can relate to her on some level. All of us have suffered a hurt or an injustice at the hands of someone else. Of course, the degree of pain will vary for each of us because the spectrum of hurts is wide and the consequences of hurts are unique. But we have all been there at some point in our lives—hurt, neglected or wronged by someone else. As believers in Christ, what do we do with the baggage of past hurts? How to we continue to walk in victory when the past seems to dog every step we take? How can we reclaim what has been stolen from us or broken in us? In the midst of being wronged, how can we be women of grace?

As always, our hope is in Christ. His Word presents principles for us to apply in the midst of adversity and hurt. When we have experienced hurt by another's hand, we must recognize God's sovereignty, refuse bitterness and release a blessing.

Recognize God's Sovereignty

The sovereignty of God is an unexplainable truth that permeates every page of Scripture. It means that God is totally and completely in control. His plans cannot be thwarted by the deeds of man. He will use the sin, injustice and hurt of this world to accomplish His will. He is in control even in the difficult circumstances of life.

For many of us, it is hard to grasp the fact that God is completely in control especially when bad things are happening. We tend to believe God is all powerful and completely sovereign, but He is not good. Or we vacillate to the opposite view, God is good but not all powerful and certainly not in control. Yet Scripture teaches God is both good and sovereign. One facet of His character never diminishes another. He is all good, all wise, all loving, all powerful and all sovereign, all the time. He never changes.

Our circumstances cannot be the filter through which we see God. If so, when our circumstances are good, then God will be good. If our circumstances are bad, then God is bad. Neither our pain nor our pleasures define His character. We must know Him based on truth not based on our circumstances. Scripture is Truth (John 17:17). The Holy Spirit always leads us in alignment with the truth of Scripture (John 16:13).

The sovereignty of God is not a place where we will find answers to all of our questions. It is, however, a place to rest and trust that God is in control even if we do not understand why things have happened. His sovereignty is not meant to alarm us or discourage us. Instead, His sovereignty is meant to encourage us. It is where we lay down our unanswered questions, and our most difficult burdens and we trust Him.

Monday, September 26, 2005 started as a joyful day. My husband, Dana and I had just returned from a weekend of working out of town and he decided to take the Monday off from his normal duties as pastor. Our youngest son stayed home with us. He and Dana were hilarious on that Monday. They played video games, ran around the house, watched movies—drove me crazy!

Later in the afternoon, I kissed my sweet husband on the top of the head as he took a break from playing. I knew Dana had a 4:30 appointment at the church and in the meantime I needed to run some errands. My last words to my husband were something about seeing him at dinner. Little did I know, on his way to church, another driver would fall asleep and hit Dana's car head on. Nine hours later, Dana stepped into Heaven. The boys and I plunged into heartache.

My youngest son came to me a few days later with brokenness dripping from his ten year old heart. He said after I left the house on Monday afternoon, his dad was ready to leave for his appointment. But my son begged his daddy to stay and play one more game. Gladly, Dana delayed his appointment for a few minutes—and played. Now, in anguish, my child wept, "Oh Mama, if I had not asked him to stay and play one more game, that car would not have hit him. It's all my fault, Mom."

I had never experienced such grief. I had no explanations for why God had allowed this horrendous loss. I held my youngest son and cried with him. My heart was screaming for answers but God's Spirit simply led me to truth. "Son, your dad's life was not in your hands. It never has been. His life has always been in God's hands, and that is where we are going to leave it."

Certainly, my precious ten year old had never studied the deep Biblical doctrine of the Sovereignty of God and yet that is the very thing that soothed his troubled mind and heart. Somehow, God is in control. He always has been and He always will be.

Listen! Bad things happen because we live in a fallen world. Yes, sometimes bad things happen as a consequence of sin or choices people make, but even then God is in control. He is always love. He is always wise. He is always good. He is always sovereign. I do not have to understand the events of my life to rest in these amazing truths. Neither must God change any circumstance in my life in order for me to embrace His love and His sovereignty. I simply must trust Him based on the truth of His Word and the steadfastness of His character.

Dear woman, you may have suffered great loss or heartache. You may have been hurt and abused by others. You may have been wronged or neglected. There will probably never be clear cut answers as to why. But rest in the truth that God has not turned a blind eye. He knows all you have encountered. He loves you and He is still in control no matter how we feel or what others do. Our response to difficulties is trusting God, a trust based on the truth—He is in control.

Jesus, I am resting, resting
In the joy of what Thou art.
I am finding out the greatness
Of Thy loving heart.[3]

Refuse Bitterness

We will never know how Tamar chose to live her life after her twins were born. We are not given any other details about her. And yet, I would like to believe, as a woman who suffered great hurt she was also a woman who experienced great joy because she refused to live in bitterness, trusting all along, God was in control.

As believers, we are admonished to refuse bitterness, no matter what heartaches we have encountered. Hebrews 12:15 is clear. *"See to it that no one comes short of the grace of God: that no root of bitterness springing up causes trouble, and by it many be defiled."* If we indulge bitterness, we are refusing to dispense the grace which we have experienced in Christ. Instead of a life marked by grace, bitterness takes root, springing up like a wild weed and poisoning everything it touches.

Have you ever met a bitter person? Maybe even a bitter Christian? You can recognize bitterness almost immediately. Cranky. Angry. Negative. Disgruntled. Vindictive. Myopic. A bitter person can make any home, church or workplace a toxic environment. They repel people instead of attracting people. No Christian should ever be viewed as bitter.

Years ago, I heard a news report on the radio. A seventy-two year old man, a retired school teacher, was arrested and convicted of stalking and vandalism. His crimes were against former co-workers and administrators who thirty years earlier had given him a negative assessment as a teacher. He had not worked with them since, but had held onto the resentment and now 30 years later was a convicted criminal. That is what bitterness can do. The Bible says dig it out. Do not let bitterness take root!

But how can a woman who has been hurt, abused, neglected or wronged keep from feeling resentful and eventually bitter? Dear woman of grace, the Lord will equip us to live in the manner which He has commanded us to live. *"It is God at work in you both to will and to do His good pleasure"* (Philippians 2:13). God says don't be bitter, therefore He will equip us to live in freedom from bitterness. But how?

The Apostle Paul had a lot of pain in his life. He had inflicted pain on many believers before he met Christ. But He had also received pain at the hand of others after he met Christ (2 Corinthians 11:24-28). Yet, Paul writes in Philippians, *"... forgetting what lies behind and reaching forward to what lies ahead, I press on..."* (Philippians 3:13-14). Whether Paul is writing about the hurts he has inflicted or the hurts he has experienced is inconsequential. He is not saying he has amnesia and can no longer remember the past. He is saying, because of Christ, the past does not determine the future.

Warren Wiersbe writes, "I cannot change the past, but by the grace of God I can change the meaning of the past."[4] Refusing bitterness is not Pollyanna thinking. Neither is it a denial of pain. Refusing bitterness is a choice we make, empowered by the Holy Spirit. We choose not to be controlled by painful events of the past. We choose instead, to trust the sovereignty and love of God with those hurtful events. We allow the Lord who loves us to take the awful events of life and redeem them, remaking them into something that brings glory to Him. I cannot explain how He does that. But He does.

Our minds are important in refusing bitterness. We cannot dwell on past events. We cannot replay the hurts over and over in our minds. Every time we replay the injustice, we dredge up the emotions that go with it. These thoughts and feelings become implanted in us, causing bitterness to set in. Scripture says we are to take every thought captive to the obedience of Christ (2 Corinthians 10:5b). Kay Arthur says we should frisk every thought at the doorway of our minds. When the old hurt comes to mind, refuse to rehearse it.[5] This is not a denial of the pain. It is a refusal to continue living in it.

Refusing to mentally rehash hurtful events is certainly a starting point but there is more. We must replace those thoughts with truth. God's Word is truth. *"Finally brethren, whatever is true, whatever is honorable, whatever is right, whatever is pure, whatever is lovely, whatever is of good repute, if there is any excellence and if anything worthy of praise, **let your mind dwell on these things**"* (Philippians 4:8). The Bible teaches us what is true, honorable, right, pure, lovely, and good. We learn by reading, studying, memorizing, singing, and meditating on God's Word. Once Scripture is established in our minds, the Holy Spirit will help us recall it and then lead us to apply it to specific situations. The implanting, recalling and applying of Scripture is what Paul means when he writes, *"be transformed by the renewing of your minds"* (Romans 12:2). God uses truth to change us and it starts in our mind.

Christians deal with hurt by first trusting our loving, sovereign Lord and second, by refusing bitterness. Refusing bitterness is accomplished as the Spirit of God uses the Word of God to reclaim and renew our minds. This is how we press on. This is the road to recovery.

I do not write these pages flippantly. I am aware that many women have suffered abuse and trauma far exceeding the imagination. I cannot begin to understand the depths of hurt some have experienced. Yet I am confident that God's Word speaks to any degree of injustice suffered. His principles and His promises apply no matter how deep the pain. He can redeem any heartache, buying it back and remaking it into something of beauty for His sake and ours.

Release a Blessing

Over and over, Scripture says we are to forgive people who have wronged us. Jesus taught His disciples that forgiveness is a necessary component of following Him. Even the Lord's Prayer states we are to forgive others as we have been forgiven. Yet forgiveness seems to be a baffling and difficult concept for even the most mature Christian. Certainly God has forgiven us, but how does that translate into the real life injustices we suffer at the hands of others?

In the New Testament, two Greek words are most often used for forgiveness, *aphiemi* and *charizomai*. I am not a Greek scholar so I rely heavily on the works of Spiros Zohdiates. Dr. Zohdiates defines *aphiemi* as sending away, dismissing: to remit, forgive debts, sins or offenses.[6] *Charizomai* is another Greek word which is translated, forgive (Colossians 3:13, Ephesians 4:32). It means to pardon, to graciously remit a person's sins.[7] *Charizomai* contains the word *charis* which means *grace*. Therefore to pardon a person's sin is an act of grace.

God is the only one who can remove sin. He not only graciously forgives us and pardons us from sin, but He also removes it and wipes the ledger clean. He does away with the debt of sin because of Christ's death on the cross. Only God can expunge sin from a life. Only God can free us from the guilt and power of sin. And thankfully, He chooses to forget our sin and never holds it against us at some point in the future.

Listen carefully. We cannot remove sin from a person. We cannot offer eternal pardon; only God can do that. We cannot release a person from the power of sin. But we can, by the power of the Holy Spirit, appropriate the forgiveness we have been given and offer it to others in the form of grace. We release, to those who have wronged us, the blessing of gracious forgiveness. In giving the gift of grace to others, we release them from shame but we also release ourselves from bitterness. It is in this atmosphere of release, the sinner sees and hears the love of God and is drawn to Him. In covering a wrong with grace, we experience freedom to walk in victory as trusting and obedient children of God.

My late husband wrote a book entitled Call 2 Ministry. In it he gives a beautiful illustration of forgiveness.

...imagine holding a small, sweet songbird with enclosed hands. Immediately you will be aware of its struggle to free itself and fly away. You have two options: open your hands to release the bird or hold on to it, trapping it in the prison of your hands. If released, the bird will fly away and your hands will be free for other opportunities. However, holding on to the bird will eventually snuff out its life and your hands will

be unusable. After the bird dies, its stench will follow you wherever you go. People won't see the rotting flesh cradled in your hands, but they will recognize the intolerable smell of death. Because your hands are occupied with this lifeless, odorous bird, you will be forced to pass up opportunities to serve others. In much the same way, we can be guilty of harboring an unforgiving spirit. On the surface, we seem to be vibrant and usable to God, but below that surface a dead, ugly, unforgiving spirit enslaves us, leaving a stench that holds us back from being the ministers God wants to us to be. [8]

Some of you are recoiling at the very thought of forgiveness. The hurts are too deep. Too much has been stolen from you. The injustices are too far-reaching. Dear one, it is not our job to heal the hurts or mend all the broken places in our lives. It is God's job. Our job is to trust Him enough to obey Him. We are to offer grace, even when we do not feel like it and even when the recipient seems unworthy and even unrepentant. Peter thinks he is being liberal when he asks Jesus if forgiving a brother seven times is enough (Matthew 18:21-22). Jesus answers with astounding extravagance. *Forgive seventy times seven.* Huh? Are you kidding? That is not only impossible, it seems a little insane. Perhaps it would help us to understand what forgiveness is not.

Forgiveness is not a denial of the pain. Forgiveness is not a "just get over it" attitude. God is not asking us to dismiss the pain. He is asking us to release the pain to Him, trusting that He is and has always been in control. We extend grace to the one who has injured us, trusting God with the outcome and trusting Him with our healing.

Forgiveness does not negate the consequences. Forgiveness cannot undo the past. Neither does forgiveness remove punitive consequences from the offender. Yet God has promised to take even the consequences of sin and use them for His glory. Our responsibility is to bow in surrender, giving Him freedom to use even the ugliest events of life for good. His grace is bigger than our choices and it is bigger than the consequences of our choices. Likewise, His grace toward us is bigger than the sinful choices others have made, choices which have adversely affected us.

Forgiveness does not guarantee restored trust or renewed relationship with the one who has hurt you. On a human level, forgiveness is not always accompanied by trust. Trust is earned; it is based on character. (That is why God is completely trustworthy: His character is flawless and unchangeable.) Time may be required if the broken relationship is to be restored. But sometimes, the relationship is never restored. Not all relationships need to be restored. The person you forgive may be just as toxic as always. They may be unrepentant. They may be abusive. God is not asking us to jump back into a harmful, toxic relationship. He is asking us to cover the wrong with grace and leave the results to Him, freeing us from bitterness. You can forgive a person and never be in a close relationship with that person again. Even though the relationship may never be restored, you can still walk in obedience and freedom. Forgiveness is more about being right with God than it is about being restored with toxic people.

Forgiveness is not a one-time event. God chooses to forget our sins and never hold them against us again. But we often remember the hurts others have caused us. If we have offered forgiveness but the emotional hurt still comes to mind, immediately take your pain to the Lord. Ask Him to empower you to take every thought captive. Ask the Holy Spirit to lead you into the truth of the Word. Be careful not to rehearse the hurtful act over and over, but give the injustice to the Lord. Keep the slate clean by refusing to continually live in the hurt. Ask the Lord to heal the broken places within you. Forgiving a person seventy times seven may be a daily conversation between you and the Lord and not a continuous verbal rehashing between you and the offender.

Forgiveness does not wait to be asked. The person who has wronged you may be oblivious to the wrong. If we wait until they ask for forgiveness, we risk becoming bitter while we wait. Perhaps the person who has hurt us is deceased or unreachable and they can never ask our forgiveness. In that case, go to God and release the memory of that person to Him, professing our forgiveness of others to the One who has graciously forgiven us. Let Him heal the wounds and redeem all that has been taken from you.

While we want to be right with others, forgiveness is primarily about our relationship to the Lord. Covering another's wrongs with grace is simply doing what has been done for us by the Lord Jesus Christ. There is healing in the release of hurt and anger. There is joy in the giving of grace.

Six weeks after Dana died, the man who hit Dana's car died as well. Authorities ruled his death an accidental overdose. This was not a bad man with a terrible driving record. This was a man who had been sick, fell asleep at the wheel and accidentally hit my husband's car. This man's death opened a whole new arena of sorrow and questions for me. How could I grieve the death of the man responsible for the horrible accident? How could I ever think of him and not feel resentment? What on earth, if anything, would God want me to do in light of yet another tragedy? I waited and eventually God directed.

In the paper work and insurance claims that follow an accident like ours, I learned that the man's mother lived close to me. He had been her only child, unmarried with no children of his own. My heart began to ache for his mother. I discovered her address among the legal papers and I decided to visit her. I had no idea what I would say or how she would receive me.

Pulling into the driveway of a modest house in my city, I was immediately met by an open back door and a terse woman wanting to know who I was and why I was there. I called her by name and introduced myself saying, "Your son and my husband were in a car accident." She began to cry and invited me in.

We sat at her kitchen table and tears spilled over from both of us. The weight of grief and sorrow shadowed every inch of her face. Her eyes could barely meet mine as she spoke. She told me of her son's deep heartache in knowing the ramifications of the accident. She relayed the hardships of his recent circumstances and she assured me he was a believer in Christ. She asked how the boys and I were doing. She wept with me again, lamenting my loss as well as her own.

I remember reaching across the table and taking her hand and somehow voicing the same words I had spoken to my son a few months earlier. "Dear woman, my husband's life was not in your son's hands. His life was in God's hands and always has been. That is where I choose to leave it."

Bewilderment and relief eased into her eyes. Somehow a burden had been lifted from us both. Our grief would not disappear, but both of us had experienced a release. She was released from any fear or guilt that might linger. I was released from any bitterness that might have settled in. We prayed together. We hugged each other. I left her home that afternoon and I have never seen her since. In fact, I cannot even recall her name.

Please understand, that dear woman had done me no wrong. There was nothing for which I could forgive her. There was no sin in her life or mine that needed to be rectified. Nothing could be said or done to change the consequences of the car accident. There was, however, a tragedy which needed to be covered with grace so two broken women could be released from further emotional harm. That afternoon...

Grace prevailed. We were both set free.

Is there something you need to release? Is there an injustice you need to cover with grace? Have you suffered a wrong from a person who needs to hear you speak words of forgiveness? Do you need to experience healing and freedom only the Lord can give?

These are not lighthearted questions. But they are questions each of us must answer and act upon if we are to live in the fullness God desires for us. You may be thinking, "Jennifer, you don't understand my circumstances. It's not what someone has done to me but rather what I have done to myself. I am the one who has caused my own hurt with sinful life choices. How can I forgive myself?"

If you are struggling with forgiveness for yourself, apply the same principles of truth. You cannot expunge sin from your life. You cannot pardon your own sin. Only God can forgive sin, making the ledger clean and He is willing to forgive you. Ask Him (1 John 1:9). Then by faith, trust that you are forgiven based on the Word of God and the perfect character of God. Live like a forgiven person, free from the guilt of sin and empowered by the Holy Spirit to live in freedom from the habit of sin. Live each day in humble thanksgiving, knowing God can use even the consequences of your sin for His glory and your good (Romans 8:28). His grace is that big, bigger than our sin and our choices.

In concluding this chapter, I find myself praising the Lord for including in His Word the difficult account of Tamar. We will never know with certainty the details of her life, but we do know she is a woman marked by grace. Even in the injustice, abuse, and neglect she suffered as well as the desperate plan she carried out, Tamar remains a chosen woman. Pursued and chosen by Almighty God to carry on the hope of a Savior. Her name is significantly penned in the book of Matthew, representing a broken life, covered with grace, restored into Judah's family, blessed with children and ultimately leading us to Christ. If God can cover Tamar's life with grace, He can cover ours as well. Recognize His sovereignty, refuse bitterness, release a blessing and watch as…

Grace prevails.

A Final Thought

Many women who have suffered abuse, trauma or difficulties may need to seek professional help as they work through painful life-events. Christian counselors, pastors, or support groups can be of great benefit. Suffering can be isolating, making us feel as if no one understands our pain. Yet God has gifted the body of Christ with individuals who understand the pain and can guide hurting people toward spiritual and emotional health. Certainly, each of us can apply Biblical truth to our circumstances but some of us may also need to seek professional Christian help.

For Group Discussion

Read Genesis 38

1. What is meant by the "sovereignty of God"? Why is it important for us to understand this Biblical truth no matter what is happening in our lives—good things or bad? How does this truth give us hope?

2. As far as we know, Tamar did not become a bitter person, despite all of the hardships she endured at the hand of Judah and his sons. Why is holding on to bitterness so self-destructive? How is toxic to others?

3. How can we prevent bitterness from taking root in our lives?

4. Why should we avoid replaying the hurts in our minds?

5. In what ways does forgiving someone who has wronged us free us from bondage?

6. Why is it important to understand "what forgiveness is not"? How does this knowledge free us to exercise Biblical forgiveness?

5

RAHAB
Living Your Faith

Faith is a word we use often but rarely define. Our definition of the word may reflect our denomination, our experience or our suppositions. For some, defining faith may be about as easy as nailing down JELLO. Yet the word *faith* is used so often in Scripture, we would do well to understand the Biblical meaning and how it applies to everyday living. Rahab is just the woman to help us.

In the previous chapter, Tamar is a woman who dressed up like a prostitute. But this chapter introduces us to Rahab who actually is a prostitute. Remarkably she is also noted as a woman of faith. How can that be? How can one so tainted by sin be heralded as an example of faith? How can a pagan point us to Christ? And why in the world would God choose to use someone like her in the lineage of the Messiah? The answer is simple.

Grace.

Who is Rahab?

As the book of Joshua opens, the nation of Israel is beginning a new chapter of history. Previously, they had been slaves in Egypt for over 400 years. God raised up His servant Moses to deliver the Israelites from Egypt. The trek out of Egypt and into the promised land of Canaan took 40 years. The journey was strewn with obstacles and disobedience on Israel's part but miracles and deliverance on God's part. Now, however, Moses is dead. Joshua is the new leader and the nation of Israel is on the cusp of moving forward into the Promised Land.

I love the book of Joshua because it reads like an adventure story. God is doing a new work in the life of Israel. The nation is moving from the disobedience of the wilderness into the blessing of the Promised Land. The first chapter of Joshua is filled with promises from God and instructions for Joshua. The land belongs to Israel. God has given it to them but now they must take possession of what is already theirs.

As the new leader, the first action Joshua takes is sending two spies into Canaan. Moses had sent in twelve spies decades earlier. It was disastrous. Only two of the twelve spies, Joshua and Caleb, brought back a good report. The other ten spies failed to understand the mission, thus giving an ominous and faithless report to Moses and the people. The bad report stirred the people of Israel to murmur against Moses and ultimately God. Israel's rebellion resulted in years of desert wandering; wandering until an entire rebellious generation died off. Now elevated to leadership, Joshua would not risk another disaster. He sent only two men.

The two spies enter the walled city of Jericho. To avoid suspicion, they go to the place where most male travelers of the day would go. They enter the house of a prostitute. The Bible uses the word *harlot* which in the Hebrew language can also be translated *innkeeper*. Many critics of Scripture have proposed

that Rahab was simply an innkeeper and not a prostitute. But
the New Testament word for *harlot* is attached to Rahab's name
in Hebrews 11:31 and James 2:25. The Greek word means
harlot, prostitute, sex for hire. There is no mistake; Rahab's job
was to please men for money.

But before we are too judgmental, prostitution was a
legitimate business for a woman in Canaan. They did not have
God's laws and certainly did not live according to any moral
standard. They were pagans who had refused to see God in
creation or to listen to the conscience He planted in every
human (See Romans 1). The Canaanites had substituted the
created for the Creator. They primarily worshipped Baal and
his female counterpart, Asherah. Worship of these false deities
included every kind of sexual perversion imaginable. Rahab
was a product of a culture without God. But that was about to
change.

Rahab welcomed the spies into her house. Joshua 2 tells
us she was well aware of who they were and where they were
from. She hides the two spies on her roof and even diverts
her own countrymen in their quest to capture the two men of
Israel. As night falls, she goes up to roof and speaks to her two
foreign guests. Her words are astounding.

Rahab the Canaanite prostitute makes a declaration of faith
in the God of Israel. She and every other Canaanite had heard
what God had done in the wilderness with His people. She had
heard of God's protection and His leadership. She knew He had
defeated armies and dried up the Red Sea for His people Israel.
News had traveled during those 40 years of desert wandering
and had finally reached the ears of a woman living on the wall
of Jericho. Joshua 2:11 is her proclamation that changes her
destiny. *"For the Lord your God, He is God in heaven above
and on earth beneath."*

It is interesting that Rahab never attended church or Sunday
School. She was never involved in a Bible Study or youth
group. There was no parachurch organization in Jericho. There

was no Christian bookstore or Christian media outlet. She just heard the news that had been traveling over hundreds of miles and forty years—and she believed it. Not only did she believe it, but she would also make a bold request based on the truth she believed.

Rahab asked to be spared when God gave the city of Jericho to the Israelites. The spies had never mentioned Joshua's plans to follow God and take the land of Canaan. But she somehow knew. She discerned the Lord God was indeed in charge, Israel was His nation and Jericho was doomed. She wanted to make sure her family was safe when the demise came. The spies agreed to deal kindly and faithfully with her and her family when Israel took the land. They instructed her to gather her family into her house and hang a scarlet rope from the window, never breathing a word of Israel's plans to anyone. She agreed. And waited.

Now Jericho was tightly shut because of the sons of Israel; no one went out and no one came in. And the Lord said to Joshua, "See, I have (already) given Jericho into your hand, with its king and valiant warriors" (Joshua 6:1). Doomsday had come. Rahab was ready.

God gave Joshua precise instructions for conquering Jericho. The men of war and seven priests along with those carrying the Ark of the Covenant (which signified God's presence) were to silently march around the city once a day for six days. On the seventh day, they were to march around the walled city seven times and the priests were to blow the ram's horn. Joshua would give the command and all the people would shout. The walls of Jericho would fall down flat.

Can you imagine the fear that engulfed the people on the inside of Jericho? For six days, a silent army marched around them. The people of Jericho were anticipating something awful, but they had no way to determine the actions of this unusual army. Perhaps they prayed to their false gods. They waited but no answers came. The seventh day heightened their fears and finally gave way to reality. Jericho had fallen. The demise of this fortified and seemingly impenetrable city came swiftly and completely. God was in charge. He had prepared His people for battle but He had also prepared the enemy by putting fear into their hearts. The taking of Jericho was a miraculous victory for the nation of Israel.

Joshua instructed the two spies to go to the harlot's house and bring the woman and her family to safety. After her rescue, Rahab lived in Israel for the rest of her life (Joshua 6:25). She did not live as a foreigner on the outskirts of camp, but she became a follower of God and found her place inside the nation of Israel. She married an Israelite man named Salmon. She gave birth to Boaz. Combining the genealogies of Ruth 4 and Matthew 1, we discover that Rahab the harlot was the great, great grandmother of King David and a woman God chose to be in the lineage of the Messiah. She is always remembered in Scripture as a woman of faith.

Grace prevails. Again.

What is Faith?

Hebrews 11:31, as well as James 2:25, states that Rahab was a woman of faith. In light of her story and these two verses, the question begs to be asked, was she a woman of faith because of what she believed or because of what she did? The answer lies in our understanding of faith.

Faith is defined in Hebrews 11:1 as the *"assurance of things hoped for, the conviction of things not seen."* Indeed, it is believing God for what we cannot yet see. It is the deepest conviction that we will receive all that has been promised to us in Christ. But there is more. The writer wants us to see faith in action. He gives us examples of people who lived by faith. Look closely at the pattern.

According to Hebrews 11, God reveals truth to a person. He gives that person instruction. That person believes God's word, trusting God enough to act on it. This is faith—acting on revealed truth. Faith is more than just believing. James 2:19 states demons believe and even shudder. But demons do not obey God. They do not act on the truth. Demons do not put their trust in God. They do not have faith in God. James 2:19 is significant because it tells us there is more to faith than just believing. Faith is belief *plus* trust *plus* action.

Faith is **not** coming up with a great idea for God and then asking Him to bless it. Faith is **not** claiming something for the glory of God which God Himself never promised. Noah did not just wake up one morning and decide to build a boat, put two of each animal in it and wait for rain. NO! **God told Noah** to build an ark, prepare it for two of every animal, and wait for rain. Noah believed God, trusted God and did exactly what God told him to do. Noah demonstrated faith.

Abraham did not get the bright idea of taking a land for God's glory and then ask God to bless his efforts, claiming it all by faith. NO! That would be presumption. **God told Abraham** to leave his family and take Sarah his wife and go to a land that God would show him. God also said He would make Abraham into a great nation. Abraham did not have a lot of specifics as to how God would accomplish all that He promised. But Abraham believed God and trusted God enough to act on what God said. That is faith.

Rahab the harlot did not just believe the news that had floated through the desert; she staked her life on it. She acted on the truth she had heard when she sheltered the spies and requested safety for herself and her family. She also acted on the truth when she tied a scarlet rope to her window, collected her family and waited to be saved. She was a woman of faith because of both what she believed AND what she did. She acted on revealed truth.

Too many times, we think being a woman of faith is for the super Christian—like the pastor's wife, or a missionary, a Bible teacher, or Christian celebrity. We often think a woman of faith is someone who attempts great and even dangerous things for God. But dear one, God has called every believer to be a person of faith. He has given us His Word to live by. When we believe His Word and trust Him enough to act on it, we are living by faith. Faith is not always the big undertakings of life. Faith is the simple walk of obedience which demonstrates we are trusting God.

That seems so simple. Unfortunately we have been led to believe a life of faith is too big and too awesome for the average believer. We have been told that if we just had more faith, greater things would happen. That is simply having faith in more faith. Faith itself is not the object. The Lord Jesus Christ is the object of our faith. We trust him. We believe Him. We act according to all that He instructs us to do through His Word and through the Holy Spirit within us.

Rahab had only a little knowledge. She had only a pagan past. She had only a limited understanding of why God was doing what He was doing. Yet in spite of her lack, she simply believed and acted, trusting God with all the things she did not yet understand. For you and me, she is a great example of faith. Like Rahab, we can exercise faith regardless of our amount of knowledge, regardless of our past and regardless of our understanding all the "whys."

Growing in Faith

If faith is for every believer, how do we get more faith? If it is not just believing harder and claiming louder, then where does it come from? How can our faith grow?

Faith is like every other aspect of the Christian life. It is given to us by grace as the Holy Spirit works within us. The Holy Spirit primarily uses two means to increase our faith. I have to admit, I would much rather grow in faith by the first means than the second.

The first means the Holy Spirit uses to increase our faith is the Word of God. Romans 10:17 informs, *"Faith comes by hearing, and hearing by the Word of God."* Our faith increases as our knowledge and understanding of God's Word increases. Henry Blackaby says, "The Spirit of God uses the Word of God to teach us the ways of God." [9] As we understand God's ways and God's heart toward us, we are more eager to obey. A person who is trusting the Lord and obeying Him is a person of faith. Only the Holy Spirt can create in us a desire to obey the Lord as well as give us the ability to obey. The Word of God is the instrument He uses to stir us and build our faith.

I mentioned in an earlier chapter, my family entertained many traveling evangelists and ministers. I always enjoyed the dinner table conversation and learned many great truths from these welcomed guests. One evening a visiting pastor and my father were discussing the topic of faith. There was a popular saying at the time that appeared on decorative posters and religious nick knacks. *Faith is coming to the end of all your light and taking one more step.*

Our guest vehemently disagreed with the popular saying. I had seen the phrase written and probably even had a poster in my room, so I was interested to hear his opposition. "Faith," he continued, "is not coming to end of all your light and taking one more step into the darkness or the unknown. Faith is taking a step into the one ray of light that God has already given." I pondered that conversation for years.

Our guest was correct. Biblical faith is not a leap into the dark. It is a step into the light. God reveals truth through His Word and we step into it. We believe it, we trust and act on it. We may not see the full picture. We may not know the ending. We may not fully understand all that God is saying or doing. Nevertheless we obey and step into the truth. Faith is very much like having a flashlight in the woods at night. You don't shine the light way out into the forest to see where you must step next. So as not to stumble, you shine the light at your feet and step into the very limited but definite light available. Psalm 119:105 reads, *"**Thy Word** is a lamp to my feet, and a light to my path."* Faith and Scripture are inseparable.

As we trust and obey the Lord, He gives us more light, more understanding of His Word. (Keep thinking about the flashlight. Only until you step into its light does it illuminate the next step.) There is, however, a responsibility on our part to stay connected to the Word. We are to abide or remain in His Word (John 15:7). When we abide in the Word, the Holy Spirit leads us into understanding and truth (John 16:13). He then enables us to act on the truth (Philippians 2:13). As we follow this process daily, our faith grows!

When Rahab is first introduced to us, she had only a limited amount of knowledge. She had only heard a few stories of God's dealings with Israel. Yet she believed and acted on what she heard. She demonstrated faith. Not for one minute do I think faith stopped there for Rahab. She came into the family of Israel and married an Israelite. She heard the history of this people. She heard the promises God had made to Abraham, Isaac and Jacob. She saw the tabernacle and the worship of Yahweh. She heard the reading of the Law of Moses. God gave her more and more light—more truth. She grew in her understanding and ultimately grew in her faith in the God of Israel as her knowledge of Him grew. She did not remain the harlot from Jericho but rather became the woman of faith hailed in Scripture as the ancestor of Christ. She lived in the new light she was being given on a daily basis. Her faith was not stagnant. It increased each day as she learned more, trusted God more and acted on truth daily.

Dear reader, faith does not grow because we will it to grow. It does not increase if we worship enthusiastically, pray louder, claim more, or believe harder. Faith grows as we spend time daily in the Word of God. Ah, we want it to be more glamorous than that. We want it to be more theatrical and noteworthy. But faith is not about us. It will never point to our great deeds and our works of righteousness. It will never be highlighted by our great leaps into the unknown. Faith is quieter. Faith is an inner journey that will be expressed in surrender and obedience, not theatrics. Faith is a gift of grace, always pointing to Christ.

The second means the Holy Spirit uses to increase our faith is trials and difficult circumstances. Oh, I do not like this way! I want still waters and green pastures. I want the way of least resistance. God, however, often chooses to grow us through hardships.

"Consider it all joy, my brethren, when you encounter various trials, knowing the testing of your faith produces endurance. And let endurance have its perfect result, that you may be perfect and complete, lacking in nothing" James 1:2-4.

James writes a practical letter for Christians. He admonishes believers to be joyful when they experience trials. Huh? How can we be joyful when life is crushing us? Let's look at James 1:2-4 carefully, phrase by phrase.

Consider it all joy... James is not saying the trial itself is joyful. Joy is an inner contentment only Christ can give. God is doing a work in us through a difficult situation. While the difficulty itself is not joyful, the fact the God has a purpose and a plan is joyful. We are to look beyond the discomfort of the trial and look into the heart of our loving heavenly Father, trusting His ways. The process, not the problem, is where we have joy.

when you encounter various trials... In the original language, encounter means to fall into unexpectedly. Not often do we plan our trials. They just happen—usually when we least expect it. *Various* means multicolored. Trials come in all shapes and sizes. Some are overwhelming and crippling. Some are the everyday annoyances of life. However big or small the trial, we rarely have planned for it.

Knowing that the testing of your faith...To have our faith tested means "put to the test to see if it is genuine." Certainly God does not need to know if our faith is genuine. But we do.

Sometimes we think we have it all together. We know all the answers. Then out of nowhere, a trial comes along and knocks us off our feet. We finally get to see how mature our faith really is. Only a difficult trial will show us the condition of our faith.

Produces endurance...The purpose of a trial is to produce something in us that was lacking beforehand. *To produce* means "to put on display." In the midst of a trial, God is doing a work in us and He is putting that work on display for everyone to see. We do not go through trials for our sake alone. Our children watch us. The unbelieving world watches us. Friends and other Christians watch. They see our hardship but they also see how we respond to the Lord during a difficult season.

During a trial, the Lord produces endurance in us. *Endurance* is a word I wish were not in Scripture. It means *the ability to bear up under.* In other words, it means God gives us the strength through the Holy Spirit to remain in the difficulty. Why, that is not what I want at all! I want out of the hardship! I want God to change things—immediately. God, on the other hand, desires more than ease and pleasantries for us. He desires a deep abiding faith and trust in Him.

And let endurance have its perfect result... God does not waste a trial. He uses the trial to mature us. He is perfecting us, not to sinless perfection but to maturity in Christ. Sometimes He leaves us in the trial for a period of time, until the trial has accomplished its purpose of maturing and growing our faith.

Years ago, our precious neighbors decided to landscape a beautiful Japanese koi fish pond into their front yard. It took weeks. They dug out a portion of the yard and fitted the hole with the perfect sized plastic pond. They filled it with water, adding a fountain that spewed a delightful stream of water back into the pond. The perimeter of the pond was landscaped with large river rocks, meticulously stacked to form a ledge. There were lily pads in the pond and ornamental yard art around the pond. And there were fish: beautiful, graceful Japanese koi fish.

One day I looked out the window to see my youngest son standing beside the neighbor's pond. A four-year-old and a new pond could not be a good mix so I called him home. An hour later, my neighbor was knocking at my door, demanding that I come and see what my son had done to her pond. From her demeanor, I gathered this was not going to be a pleasant experience.

My little four-year-old darling had done what any boy would do with water surrounded by rocks. He delightfully crashed the huge river rocks into the small plastic pond. Consequently, the fountain no longer spewed water. The lily pads were broken. The yard art was overturned. And the fish were nowhere to be seen!

"We can't find the fish!" my neighbor reported.

"Well, he didn't bring them home." I felt sure.

My distraught neighbor continued, "Koi fish are prone to heart attacks in stressful situations."

Inwardly, I rolled my eyes, thinking, they are just fish for heaven's sake.

My attitude, however, changed when she added, "...and they cost thirty five dollars each!"

I scrambled toward the pond, shouting, "Move over, friend! I am going to find those fish and do CPR!"

We found the fish. They were hiding under the rocks. Apparently, none of them suffered heart attacks. A hundred apologies and a hundred dollars later, the pond, as well as the relationship, was restored.

I learned a lot that day about neighbors and ponds and koi fish. I learned that if you purchase a small koi fish and place it in a small pond, it will remain a small fish. But you can purchase the same small koi fish and put it in a large pond and it will grow up to two feet in length. It grows in proportion to the size of its pond.

So does our faith.

If God allowed us to stay in small comfortable ponds all of our lives, our faith would remain small. Instead, sometimes He allows us to be tossed into the big overwhelming ponds of life. While it is harrowing and maybe uncomfortable, it is where our faith grows. It is in the big ponds of trials and difficulty we are tested and endurance is produced. It is where the world watches our struggles and our victories as well as our response to the Lord. In the big ponds, we are matured and perfected in our faith.

The Lord is not arbitrary in His dealings with us. He is not zapping us with difficulties just to prove a point or teach us a big lesson. He is our loving Heavenly Father who desires more than anything, Christlikeness and childlike trust from His followers.

I sat with a young widow at a women's retreat I was leading. She had only been married five months when she and her husband were in a terrible car accident. He was killed. She was injured, but survived. She wept as she talked with me.

"Jennifer, people keep telling me I am going to learn so much through this terrible experience. But am I so stupid that this is what it takes for God to teach me something?"

I cried with her. I knew exactly what she meant. People told me the same things when my husband was killed. They told me God was teaching me and they quoted Romans 8:28, spouting platitudes about it all being good. But it was not good. Death and grief and fear are not good. In fact, it was all perfectly awful.

Dear one, if you are facing a difficult trial, listen carefully. God does not allow trials in order to teach us great lessons. He allows trials in order to reveal His great presence. As He reveals Himself, we learn to trust Him and lean into Him when life hurts. The trial is not good. The problem is not joyful. But the process of leaning on, clinging to, trusting in the Lord Jesus Christ through the storms, deepens our faith as nothing else can.

I have discovered in the storms, the Lord Jesus never lets go of us. He holds us when we have no strength. He knows we are vulnerable in the storms of life. He knows our faith can be weak in times of duress. Even John the Baptist struggled with faith. Luke 7:18ff recounts John's imprisonment. While in prison it seems John becomes disheartened. He doubts. He sends for two of his disciples and tells them to find Jesus. They are to ask Jesus if He really is the Messiah or is there someone else coming?

How could John the Baptizer ask such a question? Wasn't he the voice crying in the wilderness? Wasn't he the forerunner of Christ? Wasn't he the one who baptized Jesus? Weren't John and Jesus related? How could he, of all people doubt who Jesus was? Trials do that to us sometimes. They make us question and wrestle with God. But God does not loosen His grip on us. He holds us, even while we wrestle.

Jesus hears the disciples of John ask their question. Instead of giving them a direct answer, Jesus begins to heal the sick, give sight to the blind and cast out evil spirits. He then turns to the two disciples and says, *"Go and report to John what you have seen and heard"* (Luke 7:22). Jesus wants to redirect John's focus—right back to truth. Jesus is indeed Messiah. Interestingly, after the two disciples leave to report back to John, Jesus turns to the crowd. He tells the crowd there is no one greater among men, than John.

Jesus demonstrates great mercy and love toward John. He does the same for us when our faith is weak. When our faith has been challenged by difficult circumstances, our precious Lord does not scoff at us. He demonstrates grace and mercy, always leading us back to truth. He builds in us again, through the Spirit and the Word, the truth of His love for us. He is a good and gracious Savior—all the time.

In Closing

Rahab is a woman of faith. She believed the truth and acted on it. She is an example of growing in truth and in faith. She reminds us that faith is available for anyone. Faith is not claiming dramatic impossibilities for the glory of God. Faith is believing truth revealed in Scripture and trusting Christ enough to obey.

Rahab is also a woman of grace. In spite of her obvious conversion, every time we see her name in Scripture, the word harlot is attached. Sometimes it may seem cruel that Scripture never lets us forget her former life. Yet, I believe, the Bible always includes her past so that you and I know there is no limit to the grace of God. He reaches to the lowest places to rescue and redeem. He loves the outcast and the ostracized. He brings them into the blessing of His family and deepens their faith. No one is beyond the reach of His grace. Not even you. Not even me.

Questions for Discussion

Read Joshua 2: 1-24, Joshua 6:22-25, Hebrews 11:31

1. Rahab heard and believed the stories of Israel and their God. She hid the spies when they came to Jericho. She was rescued when Jericho fell. She is described in Hebrews as a woman of faith. Was Rahab a woman of faith because of what she believed or what she did? Explain your answer.

2. Is a life of faith reserved for only a select group of believers? Why or why not?

3. How does our faith increase? (Romans 10:17 and James 1:2-4) What practical steps can we take to grow in faith through the Word of God?

4. How do trials deepen our faith? Can you recall a time when you experienced God at work through difficult trials? How did the difficulty affect your faith?

5. Throughout Scripture, Rahab's name always reminds us of her past. Why does the Bible's inclusion of "the harlot" give hope to everyone?

6

RUTH
Redeeming the Ashes

If only one word could be used to describe the story of Ruth, it would be the word *redemption*. Her story is indeed one with a happy ending, a winning against the odds. The Old Testament account of Ruth is a love story with far reaching effects. To her culture, she is the unimportant, overlooked underdog but to merciful God she is the next step toward the Messiah. Her life is a testimony of God's grace, a grace that redeems hopeless causes.

The historical setting for the book of Ruth is the time of judges. The people of Israel have occupied Canaan. The land has been dispersed to tribes and then family groups. Israel does not have a king and the period is best described by the words, *"everyone did what was right in their own eyes"*

(Judges 21:25). A new generation disregards the Lord, and consequently becomes caught in a grievous cycle. They sin and God allows an enemy to oppress them. Israel cries out to God and God then raises up a judge to deliver His people. The entire book of Judges is the telling of this cycle, over and over.

Yet within the cycle of sin, oppression, repentance and rescue, God lets us see into the lives of women who have no voice and no hope in their culture. God is their champion and He is their provision. He takes the ashes of life and turns them into a thing of beauty. For Ruth not only does grace prevail,

Grace redeems.

Understanding the Law

Before we can fully appreciate the story of Ruth, we must examine two ancient laws which provide the framework for her account. The first is *levirate marriage* (Deuteronomy 25:5-10). We discussed this law in length when we studied Tamar. It is a difficult concept for modern minds to understand. We have no correlation to levirate laws and customs. The word levir is Latin for "a husband's brother." It states that a woman who becomes a widow with no children must marry her late husband's brother. That brother produces a child with the widow in the name of his dead brother. The firstborn son is the heir of the dead brother. The child is the hope for continuing the family name as well as securing the family's possessions.

Yet another reason the law existed was God's use of it to provide for women. There was no Social Security, no pension system, and no government help for a woman in that day. A woman was dependent on her husband or her children for her livelihood, especially in her old age. Families provided for one another. Once a woman joined a family by marriage, she was the responsibility of that family until the day she died. If she became a widow, she could not remarry outside of her late husband's family but neither could she be disowned by them.

The second law is the *law of redemption* or the *law of the kinsman redeemer.* Leviticus 25:25-28 states that if someone becomes so poor that they must sell a piece of property, a kinsman has the right to purchase that property, insuring the property never leaves the family.

Again, this is a difficult concept for us to understand. To the Israelites, the land was a sacred trust. While decades earlier the land had been divided among tribes and families, the land actually belonged to God. Each family was a steward or caretaker of their portion of land. The people were not to steal or illegally obtain property as a result of someone else's dire circumstances. The abuse of land ownership is one reason God judged Israel later in their history.

The word *redeem* or *redeemer* is used 118 times in the Old Testament. The most often used form of the word is *Ga al.* It means kinsman redeemer or close relative. Every time it is used in Scripture it speaks to a situation wherein a person or a possession is in the power of another, helpless to procure their own release. A third party must intervene to win the release or buy back the person or property. The third party is the kinsman redeemer.

The kinsman redeemer must meet three qualifications. First, the redeemer must be a blood relative. Second, the redeemer must have the ability and the means to pay the price required for redemption. Finally, the redeemer must be willing to redeem his fellow kinsman. With a basic understanding of the culture and the laws of the day, the story of Ruth will make more sense. Through her story, we will also see God as the provider and redeemer He has always been. Simply by grace.

The Tender Story

Bethlehem was experiencing a famine. In an effort to find food, a man named Elimelech, his wife Naomi and their two sons Mahlon and Chilion move to the pagan land of Moab. God never intended for His people to leave their land in search of provision. His intention was that the Israelites turn to Him for their needs. For whatever reason, Elimelech took his chances with the pagans. Perhaps the plan was to stay only for a while. But the stay lasted ten years during which both sons married Moabite women, a practice forbidden by God. During the course of their stay in Moab, Elimelech dies, leaving his wife Naomi a widow. Soon thereafter both sons die, leaving two daughters-in-law, Ruth and Orpah, widowed as well.

Three women with no husbands and no children would be considered destitute in that day. There is no hope for their future and no way to take care of themselves, other than to live as paupers, always at the mercy of others. Naomi is responsible for these younger women and yet she has no means to care for them.

Word reaches Naomi that the famine in Bethlehem has ended. God has visited His people and food is now plentiful. She decides to return home but the dilemma of her two daughters-in-law presents a problem. Naomi cannot care for them. She has no younger son to give either of them in marriage (levirate marriage). The family property in Bethlehem had evidently been mortgaged or lost before they left home.

Naomi doesn't have the means to redeem it. But perhaps the greatest obstacle is the heritage of the two young women. They are Moabites, pagans, outsiders to the people of God. They would not be warmly received in Bethlehem.

In light of her plight, Naomi begs her daughters-in-law to return to their families. She urges them to find husbands among their own people, have children, be happy and leave her to her own miserable future. The younger women are under no obligation to Israelite laws. They can return to their families with no sense of responsibility or guilt. In fact one of them does just that. Orpah kisses Naomi goodbye and walks off the pages of Scripture, back to her pagan family, never to be heard of again. Ruth, however, refuses Naomi's plea.

The words Ruth speaks to Naomi in Ruth 1:16 -17 are perhaps the greatest declaration of faith and devotion found in the entire Old Testament. She is testifying of her devotion to Yahweh as well as her devotion to Naomi. These verses are often repeated in wedding vows today. I spoke them to my late husband during our wedding ceremony. This passage of Scripture still moves me.

"Do not urge me to leave you or turn back from following you; for where you lodge, I will lodge. Your people shall be my people, and your God, my God. Where you die, I will die and there I will be buried. Thus may the Lord do to me and worse if anything but death parts you and me" (Ruth 1:16-17).

Naomi has been given a wonderful gift. She has the loyalty and devotion of her young, industrious daughter-in- law. She has gained a helper and a friend. Yet Naomi chooses to see her life as unfulfilled and bitter. She blames God for her misfortune. When she returns with Ruth to Bethlehem, the women of the city can hardly believe this is the once pleasant, happy Naomi. The ten years in Moab have made her hard and sour. Naomi even calls herself Mara, meaning bitter. God, she reasoned, is against her.

Have you ever felt like Naomi? You can't seem to catch a break? Life has been one series of catastrophes after another? Things have not turned out as you planned? In such difficult circumstances it is easy to lose sight of hope. I've been there. I did not anticipate being a widow at 45 and raising two sons without their father. Neither did I foresee the challenges of remarriage and blending families. Eight years later, I certainly never expected cancer to invade my life. No, life has not turned out as I planned. At times, hope has been evasive and seemingly nonexistent. But God has never let go of me. He would not let go of Naomi and He will not let go of you either. He is the redeemer of all things broken and unfulfilled. As we surrender our broken hearts and unfulfilled plans, He buys back and makes new all that we give Him. He may not restore everything to its original order or plan but He makes us into a thing of beauty that glorifies Him.

Chapter two of the book of Ruth begins with tantalizing foreshadowing, especially if the reader is familiar with the kinsman redeemer law. Something is stirring. God is at work. Hope is on the horizon for these two destitute women.

Ruth asks Naomi if she can go out to the barley fields and glean barley so that the two of them can have food. Early in Israel's history God made provision for the poor. Whenever a harvest was reaped, the people were to leave the corners of the field for the poor. The people were also to leave gleanings for the poor to pick up and use as food. Deuteronomy states that God indeed cares and provides for the fatherless, the widow and the alien. Ruth fit this category perfectly (Deuteronomy

10:18). She takes God at His word, and goes out to gather His provision for her and Naomi. Already she is demonstrating faith.

Scripture tells us Ruth happened to go to the field of Boaz, a man of great means and a member of Elimelech's family. As she is gleaning, Boaz happens to come to the field and sees her. Make no mistake; coincidence has no place in this story. Sovereign God is at work, weaving daily matters into His divine plan. There is great comfort and hope in this truth. God is not idle as we move through our day. He is orchestrating all of our circumstances for His purposes. Our responsibility, like Ruth, is to walk by faith, obeying His Word and trusting His provision.

The conversation that ensues between Boaz and Ruth is tender. Boaz has heard of Ruth. He knows she is a Moabite but he also knows she has left her own family in order to care for her mother-in-law and honor her late husband's family. Boaz understands that Ruth has put her trust in the God of Israel. The kindness offered by Boaz is met by the thankfulness and humility of Ruth. These two people are precious.

Boaz takes the initiative, instructing Ruth to glean only in his fields. He will provide water when she is thirsty. She will sit at his table and eat with him. He will instruct his workers to leave extra gleanings for her. He gives the order that she is to be protected and free from cruelty and insults. He promises her these blessings for today and every day she returns to his fields. Ruth is overcome with thanksgiving. Boaz is gladdened by her acceptance of his goodness. Dear reader, are you catching a glimpse of the Redeemer?

On a purely human level, we don't know much about Boaz. We can know some things based on Scripture and employ our sanctified imagination for the rest. The Bible says Boaz is a man of means. He is rich. He has done well with his assets and uses them for good. He is generous and kind. He is older and evidently has no wife or children. It is here I begin to imagine.

Perhaps Boaz is less than handsome. Maybe is he extremely shy around women. It could be that he is such a diligent businessman, the years have simply slipped by and after a while he learned to be content alone. Perhaps he gave up on marriage and family after he reached a certain age. Whatever the unknown details may be, my heart settles on the fact that sovereign God saved this unclaimed blessing named Boaz for lovely, young Ruth.

On the eve of that first day of gleaning, Ruth takes her grain home to Naomi. It is enough to feed both of them! Naomi learns that Ruth has been to the fields of Boaz. She knows the law of the kinsman redeemer. She knows Boaz is a close relative of her late husband. The wheels begin to turn in Naomi's head. A plan begins to take shape. Hope begins to dawn on the distant, forgotten horizon of her bitter heart. Naomi waits for just the right moment to disclose her plans to Ruth. God has already prepared the way. Redemption is at hand.

Naomi's plans are certainly unconventional. She tells Ruth to go at night to the threshing floor. Boaz will be winnowing grain that night and when he has finished his work, he will sleep on the threshing room floor. Naomi instructs Ruth to look good and smell even better. Naomi knows that Boaz is a kinsman but she also knows he is a man. When Boaz lies down to sleep, Ruth is to secretly slip in, uncover the feet of Boaz and then quietly lie down. In essence, Ruth will be proposing.

After a hard day's work, a good meal and a little wine, Boaz settles down to sleep. Sometime in the night he feels a draft and notices his feet are exposed. He is startled to find a person lying at the foot of his pallet. He demands to know who is there. Ruth softly answers in the dark, *"I am your servant Ruth."* Boaz is fully alert and listens to her request. She asks that he put his covering over her since he is a close relative. She is asking him to marry her. Marriage would be the means of redeeming her, protecting her permanently, and providing for her future as well as Naomi's.

Could it be that Boaz is grinning from ear to ear, absolutely quivering with delight? This older man has not felt so young and excited in decades. A beautiful virtuous woman has asked him for marriage. He knows the law. He knows he has the right to redeem the lost property of Elemilech as well as marry Ruth. He also knows there is another relative, a closer relative who has the same rights. Boaz is excited about his prospects but he is more concerned about the welfare of Ruth. He wants her future secured either by him or another relative. He tells Ruth to lie down and wait until morning. He will figure this thing out quickly. I am pretty sure Boaz did not sleep a wink.

Before sunrise, Boaz gives Ruth six measures of barley and sends her home. Naomi is waiting for her. These women must have been talking like school girls about the night on the threshing room floor. Ruth is excited and nervous. Naomi is confident. She knows Boaz will not rest until the matter is settled on that very day. The redeemer is on the move!

Boaz did not become a good businessman by chance. He knew how to work with people. He knew how to make a deal and seal a deal. While Ruth is waiting to see how the rest of her life unfolds, Boaz sits down by the city gates with ten city elders, witnesses for what is about to transpire. The other close relative passes by and Boaz asks him to sit and discuss family business.

Boaz begins the conversation with land acquisition. Naomi's land either must be sold or has already been sold and must be bought back. Boaz offers the land to the nearer relative based on his position in the family. The relative says he will redeem or buy the land. Wise Boaz seems relieved but immediately lets the relative know there is a catch in the deal. The land also comes with a woman, the Moabite woman Ruth, widow of the firstborn son of Elemilech. She must be redeemed as well.

The relative back peddles. No thanks. He can't marry Ruth lest his own inheritance be jeopardized. Maybe he already has a wife and a firstborn son. Any child he would have with Ruth would inherit a portion of his estate as well. "Uh uh. No thanks. She is all yours, Cousin Boaz!" Boaz probably nonchalantly shrugged his shoulders as if to say, "Well, if you insist." The two men symbolically sign a contract by exchanging shoes and Boaz announces his intentions to redeem the land as well as marry Ruth. Bethlehem is abuzz with excitement.

Boaz and Ruth marry. God soon blesses their home with a son named Obed. Naomi's callous heart has never been softer and more thankful than when she holds that precious grandson in her arms. The women of Bethlehem remind Naomi that through this little boy, God has given hope for her future. The beauty of redemption continues as the lineage of Obed unfolds. Through Obed, Naomi will be related to King David. Ruth, the outsider, the Moabite, will be the king's great grandmother. In addition, Ruth's name will be forever linked with a royal lineage. She is listed in the genealogy of the Messiah, her life forever pointing the way to Hope.

Grace covers this entire account. Only God could redeem the ashes of these two women's lives. Only God could reach down to weary and destitute women and provide for their future so abundantly. Boaz is God's provision. He is the kinsman redeemer. Boaz meets every qualification required by law to redeem that which is lost or in the possession of another. But lest we get stuck in fairytale mode, we must understand that Boaz is more than a prince on a white horse recusing the damsel in distress. He is a picture of our Redeemer, the foreshadowing of Christ. The history of the Old Testament always points us to the fullness of the New Testament. Jesus Christ is our Redeemer and He fulfills every requirement of the law.

Our Need for a Redeemer

Scripture is clear. We are in need of a redeemer. We came into this world separated from God. Certainly, every person is created by God. Every life has value. But because of sin, people are spiritually dead to God. The first humans, Adam and Eve, chose sin. They chose to disobey their Creator and Father. Genesis 3 tells us their choice ushered in death, not only spiritual death but physical death as well.

The apostle Paul helps us understand the ramifications of Adam and Eve's choice for us today. We have inherited the nature, the bent, of our ancestor Adam. Through Adam's sin, all of mankind has been affected (Romans 5:18). We all are sinners (Romans 3:23). Please note, we do not become sinners when we commit our first act of sin. We are born sinners by nature; therefore we commit acts of sin.

Paul further clarifies our sinful condition in Ephesians. Paul also identifies himself with this sinful condition. *"And you were dead in your trespasses and sins...living is the lusts of our flesh, indulging the desires of the flesh and of the mind, and were by nature children of wrath"* (Ephesians 2:1-3). Paul also describes our broken state as *"having no hope and without God in the world"* (Ephesians 2:12).

You may be thinking, "Wait a minute. I am not nor have I ever been a bad person!" In fact you may be recounting your righteousness at this very moment. Perhaps you have been a faithful church member. Perhaps you are generous with money and give of your time as well. You are the best person you know how to be and by most standards, you are better than just good.

On the other hand, some of you may be reading this and recounting your awful, sinful choices. You may be in full agreement with Paul's description of a person without Christ. You see yourself as hopeless and cut off from God. You know the mess you have made of life and you are not sure there is life or hope or help anywhere to be found.

Let me present two illustrations. The first one is from an unknown source and I am not at all sure it is true. Nevertheless, it makes a point. The second story is my personal account.

Once there were two men who were neighbors. One man had a valuable hunting dog. The other man had a prize Angora rabbit. The neighbor with the rabbit built a little hutch in his fenced backyard for the rabbit to live in. The man with the rabbit loved his soft, beautiful rabbit and he took great pride in its beauty. The other neighbor had a fence as well but it was built to restrain his dog which seemed determined to hunt and kill the beautiful Angora rabbit.

One day, the man with the dog walked into his fenced backyard. He noticed his dog had dug a hole under the fence and into the neighbor's yard. He was horrified to see his dog lying in the yard with that beautiful Angora rabbit. To the dog owner it was obvious; his dog had killed the neighbor's rabbit and dragged it under the fence back into his own yard.

The man with the dog panicked! He took the dead rabbit into his house. He washed it. He dried and fluffed the thick, beautiful fur. He positioned the stiff, dead body of the rabbit into a lifelike pose. He quietly sneaked into his neighbor's yard and put the dead (but beautiful) rabbit back into its hutch. He then went home to wait.

Later that afternoon, the man with the dog heard his neighbor crying out, "Oh no! Oh no! Oh no!" Suspecting his rabbit-loving neighbor had discovered the dead rabbit, the dog owner innocently meandered into the back yard.

"What's the matter, neighbor?" asked the dog owner.

"It's my rabbit!" the bereaved man cried. "It died two days ago. I buried it in my yard and now it is back in the hutch!"

The first story brings a chuckle. The second story rarely brings a laugh.

When my boys were younger, a small black cat took up residency at our house. I asked the boys not to feed the stray cat but of course they did. The cat stayed and the boys became attached to her. I noticed the stray, skinny cat growing plump. She was pregnant and ready to deliver any day. Unfortunately, the little pregnant cat was hit by a car, right in front of our house.

It was not a lovely death. In fact, it was so grotesque, I called my husband at work. I asked if he would come home and scrape the remains off the street and bury it before the boys returned home from school. My sweet husband came home, shoveled the mangled remains of the dead pregnant cat into a wheel barrel and buried it in the back yard. Problem solved, right? Hardly.

Several days later I notice, bits and pieces of stinking, rotten cat all over the back yard. The neighborhood dogs had discovered the shallow grave and dug up the decaying remains of the cat. Once again, we shoveled whatever was left of the cat into a deeper hole. Gagging, we covered it with dirt and rocks, trying to secure the filthy remains once and for all.

Now that you have read two very different stories here is a question to ponder. Which one is more dead, the beautiful rabbit or the mangled cat?

Surprisingly, both are equally dead. The only difference is the degree of decay.

We all come into this world dead in our trespasses and sin. We are all equally dead. Some people, however, are like the beautiful rabbit. They are religious and moral and upstanding people but they are without Christ. They are indeed dead in their sin but they are the beautiful dead. Other people are like the cat. Sin has ravaged them. They are beaten up, dirty, ruined and seemingly hopeless. They too are dead in their trespasses and sin. They are the ugly dead. The only difference, however, in beautiful spiritually dead people and ugly spiritually dead people is the degree of decay.

Listen carefully. Whether you have been a moral, upstanding church goer or whether you have been ravaged by the effects of sin, the truth remains—dead is dead. We cannot bring ourselves back to life. We cannot lift the curse of Adam's sin. We cannot save ourselves. We need a Redeemer and His name is Jesus!

Jesus, Our Redeemer

Jesus had no intention of doing away with the Old Testament Law. In fact, he clearly states that He came to fulfill it (Matthew 5:17). The law of the kinsman redeemer is a perfect example of Jesus fulfilling the Law with Himself. He meets every qualification of the redeemer established by God in the Mosaic Law.

First, the kinsman redeemer had to be a blood relative. Jesus fulfilled this requirement when he was born of a human mother and choose to dwell in an earthly body. He became one of us. He was God with skin on. John describes Jesus as the Logos or Word. It means Jesus is the fullest expression of God Himself. When we look at Jesus, we are seeing God (John 1:1). John goes on to say, *"And the Word became flesh and dwelt among us and we beheld His glory..."* (John 1:14). Jesus is fully God but He is also fully man. He took on flesh and allowed human blood to run through His veins so that He would be related to the human race. By this kinship of blood, Jesus meets the first qualification of the kinsman redeemer.

Second, the kinsman redeemer must have the ability or the means to pay the price of redemption. For Ruth, the price of her redemption was the cost of the land. For our redemption, the price is much higher. Our redemption from the slavery of sin requires a blood sacrifice.

From the beginning of time, a life had to be given and blood had to be shed to cover sin. The wages of sin has always been death (Romans 6:23). Mercifully, God covered Adam and Eve with the skin of an animal after they sinned. That animal's life had to be sacrificed for the skin to cover their nakedness. Blood represents life, therefore blood had to shed (Genesis

3:21). Also in mercy, God later provided the Old Testament sacrificial system of killing a spotless lamb once a year to atone for sin. Again, life had to be given; therefore, blood had to shed (Leviticus 17:11). Remember! Everything in the Old Testament points us to the New Testament. That Old Testament sacrificial system is a foreshadowing of Christ. It is pointing us to Jesus. Jesus came to be the fulfillment of the Old Testament system.

Jesus is the spotless lamb pictured in the Old Testament. We do not need land and family property redeemed as did Ruth and Naomi. We need our very lives redeemed from the sin that separates us from God. Jesus had the means to pay the price of redemption. Jesus had human yet divine blood running through His veins. He was perfect, sinless in every way. He was God therefore he met every requirement of God. Jesus had the ability to pay on our behalf the price of redemption. But would He?

There was a kinsman in the story of Ruth that was related by blood and had the means to redeem the family property. He chose, however, not to exercise his right of redemption. He did not want Ruth as a wife. But Boaz wanted Ruth more than he wanted any piece of land or property. Out of love for Ruth, Boaz gladly, even triumphantly, exercised his right of redemption. He met the third requirement of the law—he was willing to redeem.

Dear reader, Jesus **chose** to redeem us! He loved us enough to willingly lay down His life for us. Not only is He related by blood. Not only does He have the ability to pay. But He willingly and graciously paid in full the price required for our redemption.

He paid the price of redemption for the ugly dead, those who have been ravaged and brutalized by sin. But, oh, He paid the same price for the beautiful religious person who is equally dead and in desperate need of a Savior as well. No matter what our state of decay, we have a kinsman redeemer! Peter exclaims, *"...you were not redeemed with perishable things like silver and gold...but with precious blood, as of a lamb unblemished and spotless, the blood of Christ"* (1 Peter 1:18-19).

I am aware we discussed redemption in an earlier chapter but its importance is worth repeating. May we never become accustomed to our redemption. I hope we never forget the price paid for our salvation was costly to Father God. I trust we will live each day in mindful thanksgiving of all that has been paid on our behalf. I hope you can envision the Father, joyfully holding us in His arms, proclaiming, "You are mine. You are mine. You are twice mine. I made you and I bought you. You are mine!"

He Still Redeems

Boaz married Ruth but their lives together did not stop at the end of the marriage ceremony. Boaz did not wipe his hands after saying "I do" and send Ruth packing to fend for herself. Life was just beginning for Boaz and Ruth. Likewise, our Redeemer, Jesus, does not save us and then leave us to our own devices. He remains. He continues to redeem all the brokenness we give to Him.

I came to know Christ at an early age. Certainly I was a sinner, but I was very young and had not been ravaged and abused by sin. There was very little evidence of decay in my young life. God, however, knew my most grievous sins would be committed long after I came into the family of God. He also knew my greatest hurts and disappointments lay ahead of me. The Lord understood the difficulties of life had not yet struck and the bitterness of grief and cancer had not yet invaded my young life. God knew that evening in Montgomery, Alabama when I first met Christ; the worst of life was yet to be. Nevertheless, He became my Redeemer that wonderful Sunday evening so long ago.

Since that night, He has redeemed sinful choices I have made and covered them with forgiveness and grace. He is still redeeming the ashes of death and grief and is giving me a garland of fresh hope. He continues to take the weariness of cancer and somehow create a daily river of joy. He is the Redeemer of all things broken and hopeless. Please hear me! He has not given back everything I lost to sin and death and sickness. Life will never be as it once was. But dear reader, God takes every heartache we give Him and He makes something new and good of it. He has been my Redeemer from an early age and He will continue to be my Redeemer until I see Him face to face.

"Do not call to mind the former things, or ponder things of the past. Behold, I will do something new, now it will spring forth: Will you not be aware of it? I will even make a roadway in the wilderness, rivers in the desert" (Isaiah 43:18-19).

Allow me to close with a few questions.

Do you understand your need for a Redeemer? Do you understand that all of us are born sinners, dead to God and unable to save ourselves from the penalty of sin? Do you know there is a Redeemer whose name is Jesus? He loves you so much. He paid the price for your redemption. He is simply waiting for you to respond to His offer.

Are you already a Christian, but life has been difficult and certainly it has not turned out as you expected? Have your plans been dashed? Your health shattered? Has a relationship ended and left you emotionally wounded? Is there anything in your life that appears to be a heap of worthless ashes? Give it all to the Redeemer.

God will not rewind the clock and restore all that has been lost. He may not remove the temporary consequences of your actions or someone else's actions toward you. He may not fulfill all the broken dreams and plans. BUT HE REDEEMS! He buys back and makes new. He somehow receives glory from all the shattered things we lay at His feet and in addition causes all things to work together for good for those who love Him (Romans 8:28).

Our lives may look very different than we envisioned. But we can say with Job, *"I know that my Redeemer lives!"* (Job 19:25) I love the story of Ruth. Not because the damsel is rescued by the prince but because the hopeless is changed by the Redeemer. Dear woman, lift up your head. Your Redeemer is drawing near.

Questions for Discussion

Read the story of Ruth in one sitting. Ruth 1-4.

1. In the Old Testament, God forbid His people to marry foreign women. Yet Ruth is a Moabite, a foreigner, who comes into the nation of Israel and even into the lineage of Christ. What does this reveal to us about the character of God? What do Ruth's words, in Ruth 1:16-17, say about her character and her faith in God?

2. Everything in the Old Testament points us to the New Testament. How does the story of Ruth and Boaz exemplify this statement?

3. Read Ephesians 2:1-5. Based on these verses, why does every person need a redeemer? Comment on this statement, "Dead is dead. The only difference is the degree of decay."

4. Jesus redeems us from sin and death but His mission as Redeemer does not stop with our salvation. He continues to redeem the hurts, injustices, and difficulties of life. Read Isaiah 43:18-19, Isaiah 61:3, Romans 8:28 and Romans 8:31-39. How can we apply these verses to redemption? Remember. The Lord does not always give back what has been lost, but He redeems.

7

BATHSHEBA
Leaving a Legacy

Bill and Opal Mattheiss are interesting people.
They are my maternal grandparents. My grandfather's family
immigrated to the United States from Germany before World
War I. My grandparents met in the panhandle of Florida where
my grandmother's family had settled and my grandfather was
in the Merchant Marines.

Bill was eleven and a half years older than Opal. He was
twenty-nine and she was a shy seventeen year old when they
met. By today's standards the age difference would be enough
to halt any budding romance. But for them, age was not a
factor. Their romance (and their marriage) lasted over fifty
years. My grandparents raised eight children and had the joy of
knowing all twenty-one of their grandchildren. Bill and Opal
Mattheiss lived full and eventful lives.

A few years ago, seventy five of us gathered for a Thanksgiving meal. Everyone in attendance was a child, grandchild, great grandchild or a relative by marriage to Bill and Opal. The patriarchal couple had long since passed away, but in their memory we began to tell stories of growing up in the Mattheiss clan. We laughed about my granddaddy's constant whistling and zippy personality. We lovingly remembered his nicknames for Opal and his talent for the violin. We reminisced about my grandmother's unmatched ability at the piano, her quiet ways and her unending patience with all of us.

But sitting there as an adult, I realized in full what I had always known in part. My grandparents were not just interesting people with a good story. My grandparents were Godly people who left an enduring legacy of faith. Every person in that room on Thanksgiving Day was a benefactor of Bill and Opal's legacy.

My grandparents loved the Lord. They served Him faithfully for decades. They raised their children to honor Christ above all else. They invested in the spiritual lives of each grandchild. Bill and Opal worshiped the Lord in the way they lived each day. They were never wealthy by earthly standards but they were rich beyond compare in things that matter.

There are not many families like mine. Every child of Bill and Opal Matthiess came to know the Lord Jesus Christ and has or is serving in some capacity in the local church. All twenty-one grandchildren have a relationship with Christ as well. Many are in full time Christian service. The legacy extends to great-grandchildren and even to the spouses of all the family. It is an incredible legacy—a lasting testimony of two people who not only lived well but invested well in others.

Our years on this earth are a hallowed trust. We must ask ourselves each day how we will invest the time we have been given. Will we leave this life simply having a story to be recounted? Or will we leave a legacy, a foundation of faith from which future generation can draw?

Bathsheba is indeed an interesting story. She has either been romanticized or vilified through the centuries. Matthew lists her in the genealogy of Christ but it seems that he does so reluctantly. He does not use her name. He simply refers to Bathsheba as *"her, who had been the wife of Uriah."* Matthew never acknowledges Bathsheba as a wife of King David. She seems to be blight on the golden boy of Jewish history. She could have been a tragic, forgotten figure on the pages of Scripture. Her story could have easily ended with despair, defeat and shame.

But Grace prevails...again.

Great Beauty

David is King of Israel. 2 Samuel 11 begins with a telling setting. It is spring, when kings go out to war. But David is weary of war. He stays in Jerusalem and sends his chief general Joab and all his soldiers to fight the battles that lingered in Israel. As the leader of Israel, David is not where he should be. Although he is physically and mentally spent from years of bloodshed, David is also, if only for a moment, out of step with God.

In the evening, King David goes to his roof top. The roof was flat and often used as a place of retreat or rest. It provided coolness in the evenings after the heat of a Middle Eastern day. It is not unusual for David to retreat to his roof where the air is fresh and the stars brilliant. It is unusual that he retreats while his armies fight without him. Perhaps he is feeling a sense of guilt. Maybe the welfare of the kingdom weighs heavy on his mind. Whatever the reason for his evening stroll, David, a man after God's own heart, is restless.

While on his roof, David sees a woman bathing. The Bible never overlooks the humanity of people. David sees a naked woman taking a bath and it just so happens she is extremely beautiful. David looks again. Many men would take a second look or at least a very long first look. We are all tempted at times. But what we do with temptation from the starting point and forward, matters. David's gaze lingers and something happens in the heart of David.

Bathsheba's beauty grabs his imagination. It is interesting how often the Bible points out the physical attributes of people. Sarah, Rachel and Bathsheba are all described as physically beautiful women. But beauty, then and now, is often in the eye of the beholder. I have no doubt Bathsheba was beautiful. But David was tired. He was mentally and spiritually depleted. That night, anyone could have been beautiful to David.

The rumbling heart of a king on the roof is a warning to all of us. Anyone who is stretched to exhaustion is vulnerable. When our mind and body is weak so is our will. Sin always takes advantage of our vulnerability during times of weariness. *It does not matter if you are a man or a woman, if you are physically, mentally and spiritually tired, anything or anybody can appear beautiful.*

My late husband used to say, "If Satan can't make you bad, he will make you busy." Busy people soon become tired people. Tired people become vulnerable and most susceptible to temptation. In no way was Bathsheba's beauty a curse. But our enemy can take any blessing and twist it to our detriment. We must be vigilant and alert. We must not become weary in the spiritual warfare we encounter daily. We must take appropriate seasons of rest so that we are energized for the battles ahead.

That night, Bathsheba was beautiful. David was restless. Failure loomed.

Great Sin

Scripture gives no indication Bathsheba knew she was being watched while she bathed. Some have speculated she seduced the king, purposefully bathing so he could see her. But the Bible is silent as to her knowledge of the king's presence or any motive she might have had for bathing in full view of the palace roof. Silence in Scripture does not always presume innocence but never once does the Bible make any moral commentary about Bathsheba. Only David is called into question by God.

The timetable for the story of David and Bathsheba is uncertain. We do not know if he sent for her that very night or if he mulled over her beauty for days. We know he inquired about her. The answers to his questions should have stopped David in his tracks.

Bathsheba, he learned, is the daughter of Eliam which makes her the granddaughter of Ahithophel, David's wise advisor (1 Samuel 16:23 and 23:34). She is also the wife of Uriah. Uriah is listed in 2 Samuel 23 among the mighty men of Israel. He is one of thirty honored soldiers who have served King David valiantly. Uriah is also a Hittite. The Hittites were enemies of Israel at one time. Evidently, Uriah was a proselyte; an outsider who had now been won over to Yahweh and His people, Israel. As king and military commander, David's obligation to Uriah should have trumped his desire for Bathsheba. It didn't. David sent for her.

Bathsheba is a young wife evidently with no children by her husband Uriah. She would be tending her home and awaiting her warring husband to return after the spring battles. When the messengers of the king arrive at her door there is no indication of force. They do not drag her to the palace. She is simply summoned by the king. How could she know what would transpire? The request to come to the palace may be disconcerting but it is exciting too.

I want details! I want to know what he said and what she said. I want to know what each of them is thinking. My curiosity wants to listen to that first awkward conversation. Was this a meeting of two consenting adults or was it a powerful king with a subservient subject? Even though our minds crave details, God does not review their sin explicitly. He guards us and the Bible simply says in a matter of fact tone, *"...and when she came to him, he lay with her..."* (2 Samuel 11:4).

We will never know if their adultery was one stolen night or if she stayed several days living in the king's personal quarters. I am fairly certain, when she returned home she did not walk out the front door of the palace. Secrecy and shame would have sent her home the back way, probably in the shadows of night. Tears may have marked her steps. The flutter of romance did not travel with her. Sin stripped her of dignity. Whether because of her sin or David's or both, shame is the covering beautiful Bathsheba wears home.

Perhaps Bathsheba thought she could put the entire indiscretion behind her. After all she is a young wife who has attracted a very powerful middle aged man—a king nonetheless. She should be flattered, if it weren't for the shame. Sin does that. What we think might be exciting, but certainly a secret, backfires. Our enemy, Satan, is a liar. When we fall for his lies, the liar becomes the accuser. Shame finds a home.

A month later, shame escorts fear into the lives of King David and Bathsheba with three simple words. *"I am pregnant."* These are the only recorded words of Bathsheba in the entire account. The simplicity of her statement speaks volumes to the desperation of the circumstances. Everyone knows her husband is out of town, fighting wars for the king. This unborn child obviously does not belong to Uriah. Adultery is forbidden. Stoning could be the penalty. Her message to David is not informational. It is a desperate, life altering plea for help. Now that he knows, she must wait for the king to respond.

David is not only a king; he is a general, a military strategist accustomed to formulating tactical plans. He kicks into action and formulates a plan based on his authority as king. He sends for Uriah. The plan is to give a trusted soldier a little R&R. Let Uriah go home, see his beautiful wife, and do what any battle worn husband does when he is reunited with his loving bride. Voila! Sin covered. Consequences erased. David's world is back in order. But the plan does not work. Uriah is too faithful to his king.

David's chest must have tightened when he learned Uriah did not go home to Bathsheba. Uriah could not enjoy the beauty of home and bride while his fellow soldiers were sleeping in an open field exposed to the elements. David tried again. Surely this soldier could not stay away from his beautiful wife for two nights, could he? David suggests Uriah stay in town one more night, hoping Uriah's desire for his wife would overshadow his loyalty to the king. Nevertheless, Uriah proved himself to be an undeterred soldier. He did not go home.

Finally David invites Uriah to a dinner. David gets Uriah drunk and then assumes alcohol will affect Uriah's reasoning for David's benefit. It doesn't. Warren Wiesrbe says, "Uriah drunk proved to be a better man than David sober, for he once again refuses to go home." [10] Darkness settles over David's soul. Uriah must die.

Great Consequences

Sin always brings sorrow and death (James 1:15). David and Bathsheba's sin would bring both. Their sin would bring the death of a valiant soldier. It would bring the death of a marriage, death of a reputation, death of close communion with God, and the death of others. And oh, their sin would bring sorrow upon sorrow upon sorrow.

The consequences of sin always outweigh the pleasure of it. David ordered Joab to take Uriah to the front lines of battle. There, Uriah dies along with other servants of David. With the news of battle, grief rolls across the home of Bathsheba and countless other widows. Death shattered happiness and normalcy for many families that day but for Bathsheba, Uriah's death shatters hope. There is no undoing what has been done. Even her speedy marriage to the king will not quiet her tumultuous guilt.

Pregnant Bathsheba moves to the palace. There is no festive marriage ceremony. She quietly becomes David's eighth wife. The legitimacy of marriage does not squelch the rumors surrounding her. Every servant whispers about the secret tryst and Uriah's untimely death. The eyebrows are raised each time Bathsheba walks into a room. David shoulders the guilt and plunges back into ruling and leading and business as usual. Bathsheba, however, sinks deeper and deeper into the darkness of despair.

My sanctified imagination believes she cried a thousand tears into her pillow each night. She yearned for life as it once was, peaceful and free of guilt. She longed to be cleansed of the consequences of her choices. She wanted to be released from the shackles of depression. Maybe the child she is carrying will bring a ray of hope and joy. Maybe God will be forgiving.

Forgiveness is always waiting but for David, repentance would need to come. The prophet Nathan confronts the king and God uses Nathan to expose David's sin (2 Samuel 12: 1-15). David's repentance is a study unto itself. Psalm 51 is the outpouring of this broken man's contrite heart. While David and Bathsheba both sinned, God placed the responsibility of their sin squarely on the shoulders of David. David is forgiven but there are still consequences yet to come. The consequences ripple outward, effecting Bathsheba, David's family and eventually the entire nation of Israel.

Bathsheba's baby is born without the fanfare and celebration of a new family member. In fact, Scripture does not even call Bathsheba David's wife but rather still refers to her as Uriah's widow. The consequences of sin are still playing out. Scripture plainly states, *"Then the Lord struck the child that Uriah's widow bore to David so that he was very sick"* (2 Samuel 12:15). Seven days later, the baby dies.

I have never lost a child through miscarriage or childbirth or at any point thereafter. I have never experienced that particular heartache—but Bathsheba did. With the death of her first child, Bathsheba plummets into a greater darkness. Defeat, despair and depression seem to be the hallmarks of her young life. Perhaps death looked more inviting to Bathsheba than life. At this point in her story, my heart weeps for her and every other woman who has experienced hopelessness. I want to cry out to anyone in despair, "Hang on dear woman! Hang on! Grace is on the way!"

Why would a loving God allow the death of an innocent child? Why would a repentant king and his new wife still suffer the consequences of sin, even after forgiveness has taken place? There are no short and simple answers to these hard questions.

God is never complacent about sin in His children's lives. He will discipline His children. Discipline is not the same thing as punishment, it is not always punitive. Discipline redirects, teaches and matures us. Discipline is a mark of the Father's love for His children (Hebrews 12:5-11). God does not want us to be disciplined and ultimately obedient so that we are mere robots. The greater purpose of obedience is freedom. He desires His children to be free from sin and its relentless guilt. He will go to any lengths to bring us into a life of freedom.

We may never fully understand the ways of Holy God but we can trust Him. We may never get answers to our difficult questions but we can rest in the goodness and wisdom of God. His promises heal our brokenness. His goodness redirects our wandering. His grace reaches into the pit and sets us on a new path. How do I know? I have been to the pit.

Soon after Dana's death, I needed legal help. I called a friend of mine in Illinois who was a deacon in his church and also an attorney. My friend gave me wise legal counsel and then said, "Jennifer, our church just lost our pastor's wife. She died suddenly of a massive heart attack. Would you mind if our pastor called you—just to check on you and the boys?"

I assumed their pastor's wife had been a senior adult—after all she died of a heart attack. I told my friend I did not mind if the pastor called me. I also assumed he was a nice little old man; a senior adult pastor, grieving as I was, for his lost spouse.

A few weeks later, that Illinois pastor called me. He was not a senior adult! In fact, he was about my age, with three children, the youngest being 8 years old. Allen and I became friends over the phone, living 360 miles from each other. Our friendship was rooted in our grief as well as our concerns for our children who were traumatized by the sudden loss of a parent. A few months later we met in person and eventually we fell in love.

Thirteen months after the loss of our spouses, Allen and I married. We married quickly, thinking we were not getting any younger. We married thinking we were giving normalcy to five children again. We married making shortsighted decisions, thinking they were best. Of the twelve people at our wedding, no one was completely supportive. My sons were begging me not to marry. My two friends assured me they would support me if I wanted to back out. My mom was a little angry. My dad was leery. Make no mistake. I married a great man. Our decision to marry was not a bad decision. Our timing, however, stunk.

After a brief honeymoon, Allen went back to Illinois and I went back to Tennessee. (We had not worked out the details of where to live.) I went to my bedroom, turned out the lights, closed the curtains, and crawled into bed. Reality had finally hit. I was married—again. I had to move my children to Illinois. I would traumatize them further. I would have to endure changes for which I was not at all ready. In light of my new reality, I could not lift my head. I wanted my old life back. I wanted peace and stability. I was grieving without hope. I was in the pit of despair. Paralyzed with fear, I simply cried and slept. For days.

Early on a Sunday morning, a friend called me. She had been up for hours, praying for me. My friend informed me, "Not only have I been praying for you, Jennifer, but the Lord gave me a song to sing over you." She added, "You know, I don't sing."

I managed a smile. "Yes, Karen, I know you do not sing."

Undaunted, Karen went on. "I am going to sing it over you anyway—because God told me to. Here goes…"

With great kindness and a shaky voice my friend began to sing. The melody of an old forgotten hymn filled my heart.

"Be still my soul, the Lord is on your side.
Bear patiently, the cross of grief and pain.
Leave to your God, to order and provide
Through every change, He faithful will remain.
Be still my soul, your best and dearest Friend
Through thorny ways, leads to a joyful end." [11]

I wept. Karen gently said, "Jennifer, get up. Go be with your husband. God will take care of you and your boys."

My pit of grief and guilt was so deep, but God's grace was deeper still. I got up. I moved my two sons to Illinois. It has not been an easy road but the Lord has indeed taken care of our family. My precious new husband has walked tenaciously with me (and our five children) through the changes. Together, we are a testimony of God's grace.

Dear reader, have you been in the pit of despair? Have you felt the weight of sinful choices or shortsighted decisions? Have you ached for peace of heart and mind? Has your story thus far been riddled with tears? Hang on dear woman. Hang on. Grace is on the way!

Bathsheba's life was forever altered. God would not rewind the clock and give back all that had been lost. Sin, shortsighted decisions, death, grief, loss and guilt had created an ugly, cavernous pit. But God would reach into her pit and give grace. Grace would have a name. Solomon.

Great Influence

After the death of her first child, the Bible says, David comforted his wife (2 Samuel 12:24). It is the first time Scripture refers to her as David's wife. The clouds of despair are beginning to lift as Bathsheba conceives and eventually another child is born. Verse 24 drips with grace. *"..And she gave birth to a son, and (s)he named him Solomon. **Now the Lord loved him.**"*

Solomon was a new beginning for Bathsheba. He would forever be a living reminder of God's forgiveness and God's mercy to her. Even Nathan the prophet joined the joyful moment when he called Solomon by the name Jedidiah, meaning *beloved of the Lord* (2 Samuel 12:25). Hope was alive in that young life. Bathsheba would waste no time investing her life into his, preparing her son for greatness.

From this point forward, Bathsheba becomes a woman of

great influence. She has more children with David than any of his other wives (1 Chronicles 3:5). It indicates a special relationship between the two of them. David obviously spent more time with Bathsheba than any other wife. She has his heart but she would later prove she also has his ear.

Years after Solomon's birth, David is on his deathbed. David is oblivious to the fact that his kingdom is experiencing turmoil at the hands of his son Adonijah (1 Kings 1: 1-10). Adonijah is attempting to take the kingdom by force. If Adonijah can establish power, he will ruthlessly kill any competition for the throne. Bathsheba and Solomon will certainly be the first to die.

God had already chosen Solomon as the next king of Israel and God had clearly revealed this to David years earlier (1 Chronicles 22). But with Adonijah grabbing power, the prophet Nathan must act quickly. He calls for the one person who will speak and immediately have the sick king's undivided attention. Nathan calls for Bathsheba (1 Kings 1:11ff).

Bathsheba is not the young adulterous woman of yesteryear. She is the queen who is respected by the prophet Nathan as well as her husband and her son Solomon. Nathan instructs Bathsheba to speak to David, asking for his help and his promise in securing Solomon's rightful place as king. She enters David's bedroom, a place reserved for the king alone. She makes her request with humility as well as intensity. Her words are wise. She moves the heart of King David to action. Her influence rescues a kingdom.

David shakes off impending death long enough to give instructions to his most faithful servants. He will elevate Solomon to king that very day. He calls for Bathsheba again. Their private conversation is moving and filled with deep emotion. It is their last recorded words to one another.

"And the king vowed and said, "As the Lord lives, who has redeemed my life from all distress, surely as I vowed to you by the God of Israel saying, 'Your son Solomon shall be king after me, and he shall sit on my throne in my place'; I will indeed do so this day.

Then Bathsheba bowed with her face to the ground, and prostrated herself before the king and said, "May my lord King David live forever." (1 Kings 1:29-31)

David honors his word. Solomon is crowned king of Israel. After David's death, Bathsheba continues to influence the kingdom through her son. Her influence is both wise and shrewd. Her last recorded actions solidify Solomon's reign.

Unseated Adonijah comes to Bathsheba to make a request. He approaches her peacefully but there is contempt in his heart. He asks that Solomon give him David's young and beautiful concubine, Abishag, to be his wife. Bathsheba must have raised her eyebrows at the request while also pretending ignorance. The request was disdainful. Abishag would simply be a trophy, a testament of Adonijah's rebellion against his dead father, David. Bathsheba agrees to ask Solomon for the young woman to be given to Adonijah. Wise and cunning Bathsheba knows exactly what her request will spawn.

The queen approaches her son, the king. He rises to meet her and offers her the throne on his right side. To sit at the right hand of the king is always representative of power. Her place of honor lets us know, Bathsheba carries great influence in the kingdom and in the life of her son Solomon. She makes the request on behalf of Adonijah. Solomon is outraged. He knows the request symbolizes rebellion and Bathsheba knows exactly what her wise son will do.

Solomon orders Adonijah to be executed along with every other leader who followed Adonijah's treasonous attempt to overthrow the kingdom. Bathsheba has skillfully yet discretely secured her son's rule and protected him from future coups. The woman oozes with influence.

Do you see the transformation that has taken place in her life? She was once the adulterous woman slipping out the back door of the palace. She was the contempt of many who saw her as blight on the king's reputation. She was the focus of gossip and stares and suggestive stories. She was the woman who could not lift her head above the grief and shame of her life. This could have been her story; a story with no triumphant ending; a story with just a fleeting whimper of hopelessness.

Grace intervenes.

God chose to cover Bathsheba's life with grace. He chose her son to be king. He could have chosen the son of another wife of David. In fact, I will never understand why God did not choose the son of Abigale. She was a wise woman who protected King David from her scoundrel of a husband. Her worthless husband dies and David swoops in to marry her. Abigale is definitely the woman I would have chosen to birth a king.

Thankfully, God chooses the least likely. God chooses the broken. God chooses women whose stories need the covering of grace. For Bathsheba, He exchanges the garments of shame and gives her the robes of grace. He allows her to influence two dynasties for His purposes. God uses her wisdom to show Solomon the importance of a mother's teaching. At least eleven times in the book of Proverbs, Solomon writes about the teaching of a wise mother. Some scholars believe King Lemuel is another name for Solomon. If that is true, Proverbs 31 and its description of a worthy wife can be hailed as Bathsheba's legacy to her son.

The words of King Lemuel, **the oracle which his mother taught him.** *.....An excellent wife, who can find? For her worth is far above jewels. The heart of her husband trusts in her.... Strength and dignity are her clothing and she smiles at the future. She opens her mouth in wisdom, and the teaching of kindness is on her tongue....Her children rise up and bless her; her husband also, and he praises her saying, "Many daughters have done nobly, but you excel them all." Charm is deceitful and beauty is in vain, but a woman who fears the Lord, she shall be praised.* (Proverbs 31:1, 10-11, 25-26, 28-39)

In light of her great influence, why does Matthew refer to Bathsheba in the genealogy of Christ as *"her, who had been the wife or Uriah"?* Why doesn't he write her name or at least refer to her as David's wife? Why does Matthew include her in the genealogy but with her inclusion remind us of her sin?

All Scripture is inspired by God. Matthew's notation about Bathsheba reminds us of God's great grace. Because of grace, no life is beyond His reach. No pit is too deep. No past is too horrific. No sin is unforgivable. Grace reaches to the lowest places. By grace, God rescues and redeems. By grace, God transformed young, adulterous Bathsheba into the wise queen who touched the heart of two kings. He turned her story into a legacy that has pointed generations to the Messiah.

Our years on earth are a gift, a trust to be invested in others for the sake of Christ. Not all of our years will be perfect or sinless, but each one can be a testimony of grace. I want my life to be more than an interesting story. I want my life to be a legacy—like Bill and Opal Mattheiss, like Bathsheba—always pointing others to Christ.

Even today dear woman, God is able to cover the chapters of our lives with grace. He is able to turn our ragged stories into enduring legacies.

Grace prevails. Grace redeems.

Questions for Discussion

Read 2 Samuel 11:1-18, 26-27, 2 Samuel 12:1-25, 1 Kings 1:11-31, and 1 Kings 2:12-25

1. Vulnerable moments such as David experienced leave us weak-willed and open to temptation. How can we fortify ourselves against times like these?

2. The prophet Nathan confronts King David with his sin. David repents but consequences still follow. Discipline is not always the same as punishment. What is the purpose of discipline? Why does God discipline His own children?
   Read Hebrews 12:7-11.

3. How does grace transform Bathsheba from a young adulterous woman into an influential queen? In spite of her past, how does she invest in her son Solomon?

   Regardless of our past, we can invest in the lives of those we love. What kind of investment are you making in future generations? Will your legacy include belief in our loving God and a relationship with Jesus Christ? If not, why not? Is it too late?

4. Read Proverbs 31: 10-31 as if you are Bathsheba speaking to her son Solomon. Which verses mean the most to you? Which passages would you like to ensure are implanted in the hearts of the next generation? How can we accomplish the implanting of truth in a practical way?

8

MARY
Facing Your Fears

Fear. It comes unannounced into our lives. It invades without partiality. It manifests itself in varying degrees, from daily worries to paralyzing phobias. Fear creates a storm of thoughts and emotions that has the potential for destruction. No matter how often it invades or how commonplace it may appear, fear rattles us. And even though the Bible addresses our fears with words like, "fear not" or "do not be afraid", fear is not something we simply get over. Our fears must be subdued, redirected and eventually replaced.

For some, it may seem odd to study Mary, the mother of Jesus, in the context of fear. For others, it may seem odd to study Mary at all. We tend to examine her life from two extremes. Either we elevate her to a place of worship never intended by God or we ignore her, fearing we will appear enamored. Often, she is politely overlooked until Christmas when we drag out our porcelain nativity scenes. But even then, she is calm and pristine, unruffled by the jarring circumstances of real life.

Regardless of our approach, Mary first appears on the pages of Scripture in Matthew 1 as the wife of Joseph and the mother of the Messiah. She is the final woman in that list of grace-covered people who lead us to hope. Given her importance, how can we put her in the same category as women like Bathsheba, Tamar and Rahab? What possible connection can she have to women like Sarah, Rebecca, Leah and Ruth? Could there be anything in her life that is lacking? After all she IS the mother of Jesus. Yet before Mary becomes the mother of Christ, she is a young Jewish girl with plans. Luke 1:26-27 gives us a glimpse into her plans.

Mary planned to wed Joseph, a carpenter from Nazareth. She planned to have his children and raise them in the Jewish tradition. She planned to love her family and see them through the joys and struggles of life. She planned to celebrate every accomplishment and rejoice in every blessing. Her plans included a lifetime of worshiping the God of Abraham, Isaac and Jacob. She would be devoted to Yahweh and she would faithfully teach her children to walk in His ways. In the end, Mary would die fulfilled, her greatest plans bearing fruit in the lives of her children and grandchildren.

Mary had a good plan. Like many women, Mary's plans centered around relationships and family. God, however, is about to alter Mary's plans. When He does, fear invades.

Great Fear

God sends an angel named Gabriel to deliver the life-altering news to Mary. The Bible says, *"And coming in, he said to her…"* (Luke 1:28). The wording of that simple phrase indicates an understated, normal entry through the door of her house. He does not alarm her with magnificent lights or blaring trumpets. He does not bring an entourage of singing angels

162

to herald the news. His appearance to Mary is vastly different from the angelic announcement to shepherds just one chapter later. No Shekinah glory, no heavenly hosts singing, no party in the sky—just a quiet entry into her life through the front door. Fear follows close behind.

Again, the Bible is understated. Imagine young Mary daydreaming about her future, mindlessly sweeping the floor or preparing the table for the next meal. Her thoughts are suddenly interrupted when a stranger comes, uninvited, into her space. We don't know what Gabriel looks like. Maybe he is taller and broader than most men. Maybe his voice is more resonate. Maybe his hair is an unusual color. Whatever his appearance, he scares the socks off of young, sweet Mary. In fact, every time an angel appears in Scripture, fear is the first response. Mary's response is no exception.

More than his unexpected appearance, Gabriel's words bring fear to Mary. He greets her as "favored one". He states God Himself is with her. Mary's mind races as Gabriel addresses her as a woman of grace, richly blessed. How can this be? She is a poor, young Jewish woman. In her culture she is not suitable for anything lofty—especially from God. Gabriel's words of comfort, "Do not be afraid," have little immediate effect.

Mary is afraid of what she does not understand. She cannot put together the pieces of Gabriel's message. She cannot fathom the reasoning behind the greeting. Her confusion creates in her an unsettling angst. The angel tries to dispel her uneasiness by assuring her of God's favor (Luke 1:30). But the words that follow his unusual greeting escalate Mary's angst to heart stopping fear.

"And behold, you will conceive in your womb, and bear a son, and you shall name Him Jesus. And He will be great, and will be called the Son of the Most High and the Lord God will give Him the throne of His father David; and He will reign over the house of Jacob forever; and His kingdom will have no end."(Luke 1:31-33)

Mary is unable to appreciate the good news of verse
32 and 33 because she cannot absorb the shock of verse 31.
She will become pregnant? Unmarried and pregnant. Pure
and pregnant. This does not fit into her plans. This is a game
changer. Why would God choose to do this? And how on earth
could it be called favor?

Charis is the Greek word for grace. The definition of grace
includes the idea of *favor*. Unfortunately, the word favor has
been abused in some theological circles. God's favor toward us
is not measured by our health, prosperity, success or position.
We cannot rely on the world's standard of favor. If we do,
when health, prosperity, success and position are threatened or
are absent, we will conclude that God's favor is absent as well.

God's grace, made available to us through Christ, is always
sufficient. It is sufficient for salvation and it is sufficient for
everyday living (2 Corinthians 12:9). His grace is enough when
health and wealth are absent. His favor on us remains even
if the difficult circumstances of life continue. Certainly, like
Mary, we may wrestle with what seems to be a contradiction
between our circumstances and God's grace. But God's grace,
His favor, is present and sufficient, even when the news is
frightening. Even when the future seems uncertain. Even when
we cannot comprehend what God is doing. Grace is still at
work because God, not circumstances, is in control.

Mary knows and loves God. But as she envisions her
future, the heat of fear flushes her face and grips her chest.
Surely this is mistake. Favor and the news of pregnancy seem
to conflict. An unmarried pregnancy will result in speculation,
rejection and loss of reputation. It will certainly end her plans
to marry Joseph. In fact, a baby out of wedlock will end every
plan! At the very worst, death by stoning could result. At the
very least, a life of shame looms before her.

Her fear finds a voice when she asks, *"How can this be,
since I am a virgin?"* Mary understands the human side of
creating life. It is physically impossible for her to conceive a

child alone. Her logic and her faith in God are on a collision course. Fear of the impossible links arms with fear of the unknown. Surely God knows what He is doing, but how will He do it? Fear hangs on while Mary simply tries to breathe.

Do you see her humanity? Can you understand her fear? Perhaps we can all relate to young Mary because each of us at some point and to some degree, has experienced life-altering news. Something walks through the door of life and changes everything. And when change walks in, fear, anxiety and uncertainty come in as well. We find ourselves wrestling with the truth of grace and the reality of difficult circumstances.

Fear walked into my life in December of 2013 with three simple words. "You have cancer." It was not what I expected but there it was. Invasive lobular carcinoma. Breast cancer. I understood my diagnosis was a game changer. Life would be forever different. And I was afraid.

So many cancer patients endure great physical battles. My battle, however, was not primarily with cancer. My greatest battle was with fear. I was diagnosed during the Christmas holidays and no doctor or hospital was functioning under a normal schedule. I would have to wait several weeks from my first diagnosis to my first surgery. During the wait, fear took over.

Like Mary, I was afraid of what I did not understand. What was God thinking? How could He allow more heartache into my life and the life of my family? What could He possibly accomplish in me for HIS glory through cancer? Hadn't we all suffered enough? Fear would not let go. Peace would not settle in. I became consumed with dread.

My first surgery led to a second, each time finding more cancer. A third surgery was in order. Fear of the future linked arms with fear of the unknown. Like Mary, I was simply trying to breathe. I wanted peace. I could not continue living in constant emotional turmoil. Fear is not from the Lord (2 Timothy 1:7). Yet my faith seemed so weak and my mind so overwhelmed with fear. I knew I was in a spiritual battle that was testing the limits and I felt like I was losing. Mercifully, Jesus stepped in. He used a friend and a song to subdue the fear and redirect me into truth and eventually hope.

Dear reader, our Lord never abandons us in our fear. Gabriel will not leave Mary to drown in her fears. He speaks peace and hope into her life even as she questions. The Lord does the same for us. He covers our fear with His mercy and grace. He quiets the storm in our hearts. He redirects our minds into truth and He anchors us in hope. Hope will never let us go because it is built on Jesus Christ. Hope anchors Mary. It anchors you and me as well.

Great Hope

Biblical hope is not wishful thinking. The Classic Greek noun *elpis*, translated *hope*, means "the desire of some good with expectation of obtaining it." [12] Yet in the context of Scripture, *elpis* carries a fuller meaning. For the believer in Christ, hope is the anticipation of a good thing and the certainty of receiving it based on the Word of God and the character of God. Biblical hope is always forward looking but includes more than our future destination of Heaven. Hope is the anticipation of receiving all that God has promised—here on earth and eventually in Heaven.

Gabriel speaks hope into Mary's life; hope based on the Word of God and the faithful, loving character of God. Twice in Gabriel's message, he assures Mary she will be carrying God's Son. Her pregnancy will not be a complicated mishap but rather a divine intervention of the Holy Spirit. Jesus, meaning Savior, will be her joy to bear. He is the long anticipated Messiah, the eternal King of Israel. Her womb will carry the hope of the world. She will be the earthly mother to the Son of God.

Mary is not chosen because she is the most qualified to

mother the Messiah. She is chosen simply by grace. God
will cover every fear and every inadequacy with His mercy
and grace. The precious young woman can rest in the angel's
greeting which at first, she did not understand. She is indeed
a favored woman of grace for she will bring into the world
the embodiment of God's grace. Jesus. Her anticipation of the
future begins to build. Mary cannot completely understand the
greatness of Gabriel's message but hope is taking root. Fear is
backing out the door.

Like many of us, Mary's fear included an uncertainty about
the future. She was looking ahead to the next nine months, the
next few years and the span of her own lifetime. God, on the
other hand, looks at the eternal future. Her child would be an
eternal king. He would provide eternal salvation and eternal
hope. His kingdom and His authority would have no end.
Mary's view of the future was limited. God's view is not. Her
fear of the future is subdued by the truth of God's eternal plan.
Hope stands firm. Fear takes another step back.

One fear remains. Her haunting question, *"How can this
be, since I am a virgin?"* Fear of the impossible must step
aside as well. Gabriel assures Mary her pregnancy will be
a supernatural work of the Holy Spirit. Not often does God
explain Himself. But for young, innocent Mary, the assurance
that God is completely and graciously in control, settles her
mind. Still, God gives her even more. God gives Mary a sign
and a promise.

In Scripture, the same sequence of events follows every
angelic appearance. First the angel appears, eliciting fear. Then
the angel offers comfort and delivers God's message. Finally,
the angel gives a sign confirming the authenticity of the
message. For Mary, the sign is her older cousin Elizabeth.

Elizabeth is the wife of Zacharias, a Jewish priest.
Zacharias and Elizabeth are righteous people, *"walking
blameless in the all the commandments and requirements
of the Lord."* The couple is advanced in years and they are

childless because Elizabeth is barren (Luke 1:5-7). The exciting announcement and the authenticating sign for Mary is the news her cousin Elizabeth is pregnant!

The impossible has been routed. El Shaddai has stepped in once again. An older woman, long past the age of childbearing has conceived. An ancient remembrance of Sarah and Abraham dances in Mary's head. The angel lays a promise alongside Mary's joy. *"For nothing will be impossible with God."* Fear of the unknown, fear of the future and fear of the impossible simultaneously melt. Hope takes over.

The promise given by Gabriel has great significance for us as well. The word *nothing* literally means *not any word.* In its most literal form, Luke 1:37 says, "Not any word spoken by God is impossible." There is boundless hope and also sobering precautions in this simple verse.

Hope flourishes because anything God says, God will do. He is faithful to His Word and His Word flows from His unfailing, unchangeable character. We can rest in the assurance of His promises. We can live in hopeful anticipation of receiving all that is ours in Christ. So what has God promised to the believer in Christ?

"I will never desert you, nor will I ever forsake you."
(Hebrews 13:5)

"My peace I give to you..." (John 14:27)

"My grace is sufficient for you..." (2 Corinthians 12:9)

"And my God will supply all your needs according to His riches in Christ Jesus..." (Philippians 4:19)

"(Nothing) can separate us from the love of God which is in Christ Jesus..." (Romans 8:38-39)

168

"No one is able to snatch them (you)
out of the Father's hand..." (John 10:29)

"In Him we have redemption through His blood, the
forgiveness of our trespasses..." (Ephesians 1:7)

These are but a few of the thousands of promises which belong to those who know the Lord Jesus. When we read God's Word, meditate on it and hide it in our hearts, the Holy Spirit begins to apply the promises of God to our lives. He directs us into truth. He brings to mind Scripture that is applicable to our daily circumstances. The Holy Spirit teaches us how to utilize the promises of God with wisdom and discernment. He also guards us from presumption.

Holy God does not allow us to indulge in wishful thinking and call it hope. We cannot come up with a great idea, claim it in Jesus name, pray "real hard" about it and then expect God to come through—on our terms. The promise of Luke 1:37 is clear. What God has already said in His word, He will do. Nothing is impossible if God has already promised it. That is a safeguard for us. We will not be disappointed if our hope rests in the faithful character and unfailing Word of Father God. Mary is anchored in hope because God is true to His Word. You and I have hope because God is still true to his Word.

During my initial diagnosis of cancer, my greatest need was peace. God promises peace for His children even in the struggles of life (John 14:27). A mind filled with anxiety and fear is never His plan (Philippians 4: 6, Matthew 6:34, 2 Timothy 1:7). My battle with fear, however, continued to rage inside of me until I felt like I would lose my mind.

One morning, I stood in the shower, crying. I was in pain. I was tired. I was depressed. I was scared. Mercifully, the Holy Spirit quietly whispered, *"Peace"*. In His gentle whisper, He reminded me of the promises of God. In a feeble effort to respond, I began to sing a chorus I had learned decades earlier.

Peace. Peace, wonderful peace, coming down from the Father above…

I couldn't remember all of the words. I knew the melody so I hummed the remainder of the chorus. Then I tried singing it again, hoping the lyrics would return to my memory.

Peace. Peace, wonderful peace, coming down from the Father above…

Nothing. I was stuck. I could not recall the last two lines. I tried to sing that little chorus a dozen times but no amount of repeating it could jog my memory. I stepped out of the shower and began to dry my hair, still singing over and over the first line of the song and humming the remainder.

As I finished drying my hair, I noticed a text message had come across my phone which was lying on the bathroom counter. The message was from a dear, praying friend who lives hundreds of miles away. Cathy's message read, "Jennifer, today I am praying this song for you… *Peace, peace, wonderful peace, coming down from the Father above.* **Sweep over my spirit forever, I pray, in fathomless billows of love"**.

The timing and content of Cathy's message was no coincidence. God had this. My diagnosis had not taken the Lord by surprise. He would walk with me through all of it. He would never leave me. He would give peace in the tumultuous storm of cancer. In an instant, peace flooded my soul. Fear dissipated as God's Word permeated my mind and redirected my thoughts. Hope anchored me. I bowed my head and wept with thankfulness.

Dear reader, peace did not come to me that morning because I was given a promise of healing. Peace did not come because somehow God rescued me out of my difficulties. While today I am thankful to be cancer free, God has never given any assurances about my future. Instead, He has asked me to trust Him daily with whatever circumstances each day holds. Peace is mine, and yours, simply because God promises peace to His children even in the storms of life.

Our hope does not lie in good circumstances. The good, promised to us by God, is not always green pastures and calm waters. Our hope is Christ. He is the basis of our access to the promises of God. He will not let us go. He is the anchor for our souls. Dear reader, no matter what fear has invaded your life, hope holds. Every. Single. Time.

Great Faith

Mary's response to hope is faith. Faith is not just a belief (James 2:19). Faith is an action. It is acting on what we believe. Mary demonstrates great faith as she acknowledges her willingness to participate in God's plan.

"Behold, the bondslave of the Lord: be it done to me according to your word."(Luke 1:38)

Mary's use of the word *bondslave* or *hand maiden* reflects her heart toward God. She is not the master of her own fate or the captain of her own soul. She is a servant of God Almighty. His will is her will. His plan will be her plan. Mary is all in. She does not set boundaries and limitations as to her degree of participation. She does not bargain for better conditions or cajole for greater importance. Certainly, Mary cannot see into the future. She only has enough light, enough truth, for that one moment—and she steps into the light God has given. She willingly and wholeheartedly submits to the will of the Father.

Oh to be like Mary! To be abandoned to the Father's will with no reservations. So many times, we want all of the answers before we submit. We want to know how God is going to work before we give up our own plans. We want to walk by sight instead of by faith. Not Mary. She simply trusted God and bowed in surrender no matter what the future held.

Mary's declaration of faith does not erase her humanity. She is not suddenly elevated to a divine position, exempt from the fears and trauma that often accompany motherhood. In fact, even as a chosen, favored, woman of grace, Mary would face numerous fears.

Fear must have tugged at her mind the night she and Joseph arrive in Bethlehem and there is no room at the local inn. The realization she will give birth to her first child in a stable with Joseph as her only midwife would give any expectant mother cause to fear! Later, fear must have accompanied the holy family as they flee in the night to Egypt, trying to escape Herod's atrocities. And what about the time she and Joseph lost track of young Jesus in Jerusalem at the Feast of Passover? Can't you imagine her motherly fear? "Joseph, for Heaven's sake, we have lost the Son of God!" Lose your child at the shopping mall—just once—and you will know how she felt!

Years later, dark clouds of concern gather as Mary hears the religious leaders question her son. She knows they are gathering evidence against Him. She feels the prickle of fear on her skin. Fear soon escalates from a subtle prickle to a painful stab when Mary receives the news, her Jesus has been arrested. As she witnesses the brutality of her son's death, fear viciously mocks her. Jesus is not just God's son; He is her son, her firstborn, the child of her youth. This time, fear joins forces with grief and together they ravage her tender heart. Finally, in the three quiet days after Jesus' crucifixion, it seems fear is the only thing still breathing.

God never expected Mary to be a stalwart rock of faith who would never experience fear again. He did, however, promise to meet her at every point of need. In the storms of life, God will hold Mary securely so she can lean into His strength and listen for His voice above the winds of fear. She will be drawn by His Spirit to the hope given her from the beginning. The Heavenly Father will equip her to respond in faith even when bad circumstances seem to collide with God's goodness.

Dear reader, God did not choose to have a relationship with you because you are already perfect. He chose each of us in our sin and imperfection. He chooses to walk daily with us through every storm. He gives us the opportunity to listen to His voice when the winds of doubt and fear howl. He lovingly anchors us in Christ. He equips us to respond in faith to the hope that is already ours. We can trust God's unfailing Word and His loving heart toward us. Fear cannot survive where hope and faith abound.

Since cancer is a very fresh memory to me, fear still creeps into my mind each time I walk into a doctor's office or experience a new pain or notice an unusual symptom. I asked my younger cousin, Michal, a breast cancer survivor as well, about recurring fear. Her reply was filled with Godly wisdom. "Jennifer, each time something causes me to fear, I view it as a new place to trust God."

The truth is so simple. God can be trusted with anything that walks into our lives and causes fear. We can live fearlessly, knowing we have hope. Hope will never let us go because our hope is Jesus Christ. My prayer is that each of us will bow in surrender and say with Mary, *"Behold, the handmaiden of the Lord, be it done to me according to Your word."*

"May the God of hope fill you with all joy and peace as you trust Him, so that you may overflow with hope by the power of the Holy Spirit." Romans 15:13 NIV

Questions for Discussion

Read Luke 1:26-38.

1. Imagine finding yourself in Mary's situation. Write down your thoughts and feelings as if you were writing in a diary.

2. Fear is not from the Lord. Instead, we have been given a spirit of power, love and self-control (1Timothy 1:7). How can we quiet our fears and redirect our minds when we find ourselves experiencing fear?

3. The word "favor" has been abused in recent years. Using a Biblical definition of "favor" how can we reconcile God's favor and difficult circumstances?

4. Explain "Biblical hope" as opposed to "wishful thinking". How does hope anchor us? How does Biblical hope guard us from a "name it and claim it" attitude?

5. Nothing is impossible with God (Luke 1:37). No word spoken by God is impossible. What are some of the promises God has already made to believers in Christ? Is there a particular promise that has special meaning to you?

Notes

1. John Newton, Amazing Grace, 1779, Public Domain.

2. Spiros Zodhiates, Th.D., Executive Editor, **Hebrew-Greek Key Word Study Bible, New American Standard Bible** (Chattanooga, TN: AMG Publishers, 1990), 1561.

3. Jean Sophia Pigott, **Jesus I am Resting**, 19thc, Public Domain.

4. Warren Wiersbe, **The Bible Exposition Commentary, New Testament Vol. 2** (Colorado Springs, CO: Cook Communications Ministry, 2001) 89.

5. Kay Arthur, **Lord, Is It Warfare? Teach Me to Stand**. (Portland, OR: Multnomah Press, 1991) 273.

6. Spiros Zodhiates, Th.D., Executive editor, **Hebrew-Greek Key Word Study Bible, New American Standard Bible** (Chattanooga, TN: AMG Publishers, 1990), 1814.

7. Ibid. 1886.

8. Dana Mathewson D.Min., **Call 2 Ministry** (Xulon Press, 2003), 66.

9. Henry Blackaby, **Experiencing God, Knowing and Doing the Will of God** (Nashville, TN: B&H Publishing Group, 2008)

10. Warren Wiersbe, **The Bible Exposition Commentary, Old Testament History** (Colorado Springs, CO: Cook Communications Ministry, 2003) 335.

11. Catherine Amalea Dorthe von Schlegal, **Be Still My Soul,** 1752, Public Domain.

12. Spiros Zodiates, Th.D., **The Complete Word Study Dictionary New Testament** (Chattanooga, TN: AMG Publishers, 1992) 570.

13. W.D. Cornell, **Wonderful Peace**, 19th c., Public Domain.

Thank You

God's provision of so many friends, family members and helpers throughout this project is a precious demonstration of His grace to me.

I am thankful for my husband **Allen**. Your constant encouragement and tenacious love have pushed me to accomplish things I thought were impossible. You are the lionhearted man God gave in the darkest days of my life. I am thankful our marriage is a testimony of grace.

I am thankful for my "first sons", **Daniel and Micah**. You have graciously allowed me to use your experiences as illustrations in this book. Both of you are a unique answer to prayer and a constant source of joy. I am sure your dad is in that great cloud of witnesses; cheering for you as you run toward the goal of the high calling of Christ.

For the three children grafted into my heart, **Laura, Robby and David**, I am forever grateful and immeasurably blessed. Only God's grace could birth such joy and hope from sorrow and loss.

Jenna, Meredith, Christopher, Cooper and Callie, you add joy upon joy and blessing upon blessing to my life. By grace, God brought each of you into our family at just the right time.

My parents, **Haywood and June Cosby**, are great testimonies of God's grace and love to me. Daddy, thank you for every investment you made in me and so many others. Your reward in heaven was certainly waiting. Mama, thank you for being an example of Christ-like service, forever etched in my mind. Through both of you, I am blessed with a Godly heritage and a gigantic extended family!

In addition to my family, church families have profoundly influenced this project and I am thankful.

Thank you, **Buffat Heights Baptist Church**, for nurturing a young pastor and his wife. You blessed us for thirteen years, through great joy and great loss. I am glad it was Buffat Heights who was there when tragedy struck. You are a testimony of the goodness of God and you are the reason East Tennessee will always be home.

First Baptist Church Cobden, Illinois loved me to healing. You embraced me during difficult years and demonstrated great grace to my family. It was with you, Women of Grace developed as a study. Thank you for friendships that will endure through the years and across the miles. Southern Illinois holds a huge piece of my heart.

Venice Presbyterian Church in Venice, Florida has proven to be one of God's sweetest surprises. You walked with me though cancer, cheering me on and holding up my arms when I became weary in the battle. *Dick and Lois Armstrong,* thank you for gently pushing me to complete this manuscript. *Gerda Robinson,* thank you for your encouragement to continue writing. *Pastor Lyn Olson,* thank you for the invitation to teach. We never dreamed at the time, such a bond would be forged.

First Baptist Church Venice, Florida is my home church. You have welcomed me and encouraged me to exercise my giftedness in the body of Christ. You have prayed with me, over me and for me in times of duress as well as times of joy. Thank you for being my church family in this unique season of my life. Thank you *Pastor Tom Hodge* for your uncompromised preaching of God's Word as well as your shepherd's heart.

In closing, I must thank the women who labored with me during the process of writing a book.

Marcia Bickmore, what would I have done without you? You proved to be the perfect first editor. You kindness coupled with your Pennsylvania directness have been a treasure. Thank you for your willingness to spend hours helping me. Thank you for your patience with a novice as well as your constant encouragement to continue. You are truly God's provision and God's gift to me while writing Women of Grace.

Thank you, **Winnie Mattheiss and Trina Aker,** for making excellent suggestions in the editing of Women of Grace. Your expertise is valued and I am deeply thankful for your willingness to help me.

Thank you, **LeeAnn Martin** for your artistic skills and your marketing talents. You have helped me see future possibilities.

The Pit Watchers. Thank you, *LeeAnn, Trina, Resa, Bethany, Cathy, Michal, the Samford Sisterhood,* and every other woman who lovingly watched over me during the difficult journey of cancer. You are the ones who prayed tenaciously for me, fighting spiritual battles for me when the pit of discouragement loomed. You never allowed me to wallow in self-pity and you constantly refocused me toward hope. Thank you. You are all women of grace.

Finally, thank you to my Redeemer, the Lord Jesus. By grace, You have reached into the pit and redeemed me. You continue to redeem the brokenness of difficult circumstances and cover them with grace. *"I will sing to the Lord, because He has dealt bountifully with me"* (Psalm 13:6).